The Five Pillars of Purpose-Driven Profit

Maximize the Value of Your Early Childhood Education Business

Kathy Ligon

Author's Note

As you read and consider this information, I invite you to use HINGE Advisors' free benchmarking tool to analyze your individual financial metrics. Go to FrameworkbyHinge.com and choose "Free Assessment." Input your school's billing cycle (weekly or monthly), licensed capacity, average tuition rate (for most schools the full-time three-year-old rate), and current occupancy. The app will populate to create a benchmark that will show you what the average financially healthy school, given your size and tuition rate structure, will spend in each expense category. The first set of columns will give you a benchmark based on the occupancy you selected, and you can use the drop-down tabs to expand each expense section. The second set of columns will allow you to adjust your benchmark at different occupancy levels. This exercise will be helpful in understanding and putting into action the Five Pillars of Purpose-Driven Profit outlined in this book. This book isn't one to merely read, but to DO!

Welcome!

I am honored that you are investing your time and resources into reading this book. It comes from a place of deep love for your life's mission and for the millions of people you collectively reach by caring for and educating young children, supporting families, and empowering teachers.

Early education providers will never know the extent of the lives they have touched and enriched, as the effect spreads far beyond those they will ever know personally. Generations after your life's work is done, people will continue to be uplifted by your work. With that thought, I honor you with this book—with great hope that it shines a light on what you mean to the world and teaches you concrete ways you can create a financially thriving organization, serving children and families in a way that provides the high-quality education that all children deserve.

As you will never know the impact of your life's work, Mrs. Harriet won't have the opportunity to know the impact she had on my life and the lives of those I am close to. I regret that Mrs. Harriet passed before I could thank her for the French she taught at Mama Frazier's kindergarten in Greenwood, South Carolina, where I had my own preschool experience. I was enthralled in French class and for many years after, practiced my French over and over, dreaming of the faraway places I might go and the people I might meet. As I recently travelled to Paris, sharing my love of other countries with my two oldest grandchildren, Cooper and Elliott, I thought fondly of Mrs. Harriet and what her simple French class brought to my life. I hope that the joy that Mrs. Harriet fostered in me will continue through my family and many generations to come. It is with great love that I have created a fictional business owner case study in her honor, contained in this book.

The title of this book, *The Five Pillars of Purpose-Driven Profit*, is the cornerstone of the teaching that I have developed and refined since beginning my career in early education in 1986. It has been a joy and a blessing to bring financial and business concepts to owners and managers of early education businesses and to help them create and maintain financially stable companies that serve their lives' mission. This material has been shared at many HINGE events, including our one-day financial deep-dive, THRIVE, and our three-day business and financial conference, SHIFT. In addition, it is the cornerstone of my teaching at hundreds of outside speaking engagements throughout the United States and internationally. Our metrics and strategies are continuously tempered with changes in the market and maintain healthy alignment with current business practices. Although this book lived in me for many years, it became a passion and a purpose when our non-profit, BOOST, was launched in 2024. BOOST is a non-profit organization designed to support the home and health crisis needs of our nation's early educators and to provide education and resources that support their personal well-being. All of the book's proceeds will be donated to this exciting initiative to help it become a significant contributor to the well-being of our nation's early education professionals. Thank you for your contribution by purchasing this book, and I invite you to continue to support this meaningful cause.

Finally, as I prepare to launch this book, I am mindful that although the Five Pillars have remained constant throughout my career in early education that began in 1986, economies and support systems will shift, and the strategies to create healthy financial metrics will evolve. My commitment is to continue to listen, create, share, learn, and support you in your mission to serve our most important learners. And for as long as I am able, I will be an advocate of early education business owners.

Kathy Ligon
August 13, 2024

Part I

Learning the Ropes

Chapter 1
Bury Me Out Back

I regularly say to young people that the point where their talent and passion meet is a unique and meaningful life experience that will bring them great joy and success. That meeting point for me began in 1986 when I encountered an opportunity to work in the early education industry.

My first exposure to childcare came a bit earlier, in 1983, when I graduated college with an accounting degree and began my career at a regional accounting firm. University was an interesting experience for me. I was a psychology major, hoping to become a therapist, when I began taking accounting and math courses to fulfill my electives. I found these courses to be "easy As," but they lacked the meaning I would eventually seek in my work. In a meeting with my academic advisor, he said that I could easily graduate with an accounting degree instead of a psychology degree, so that's what I did! I did not realize at the time that they would both eventually serve me well in my work.

When entering the workforce, I began searching for care for my two-year-old daughter, trying several less-than-great options before finding a local multi-site childcare company that seemed a good fit. My introduction to the economics of the industry began with me counting the little heads in my daughter's class, multiplying that number by the $45 weekly tuition that I was paying for full-time care, and concluding that the owners were making a fortune! I regularly tell this story as a funny illustration of the lack of knowledge and information among parents—even this one, an accountant—around the economics of childcare. Educating consumers (parents and guardians) about the true economics of our industry offers a great opportunity, so more on that later.

The several years I spent in public accounting provided exposure to many types of accounting—payroll, bookkeeping, tax, audit, fiduciary—and I enjoyed the work and the people. On Christmas Eve in 1985, I welcomed a second child, a son. If you are familiar with public accounting and tax preparation, you can imagine the workload I returned to six weeks later as a mom to a four-year-old and a six-week-old. Tax season at the time, and often today, meant the expectation of fifty to sixty hour work weeks, and as you can imagine, it was a brutal couple of months. In my young career, with few women breaking into the accounting industry, I was grateful for the opportunity, and it never occurred to me to ask for a different situation that might better support me, my family, and my well-being. If I had even imagined the possibility and been brave enough to ask for it, I have no idea how that request would have been received at the time. At the end of the day, my family depended on my income, so economically it may not have even been possible.

After surviving that tax season, I heard that the now five-site early education group where my children went to school was looking for someone to do their financial work. Fully intending to go back to the public accounting position I loved after spending a few years with this "little preschool company," what I found instead was a growing industry full of opportunity and excitement. I saw the ability to use my accounting skills for something purposeful and fell in love with the people and their mission-driven work. The brief time I meant to be there before returning to public accounting turned into seventeen years, and I had the unique opportunity of advancing from a financial role (along with anything else that needed to be done!), to an operations role, and then to a growth role, where I found my deep love of the industry.

And so, my journey began. It quickly became evident that there was nowhere to find industry information about what healthy financial performance looked like or how to navigate a business that could create the necessary resources required to provide high-quality education. It seemed to be an industry that was meaningful, fast-growing, and full of opportunity, and I discovered my own ability to contribute by creating and training teams in business and financial concepts and practices. This training was largely for educators who were dedicating their lives to supporting young children and their families. Most had not had access to training in business concepts. It was here that I saw an opportunity to support and create. And the idea that $45 a week in tuition was highway robbery? Well, that went away VERY quickly.

I learned how to manage growth as we grew the company from five to around 120 schools over the seventeen years I was there. I navigated the growth of systems such as teams, logistics, financial, operational, and quality control. I was able to experiment with people management by adding support teams and developing infrastructure. I had the unique opportunity to meet business owners wanting to sell their schools, focusing on their objectives and creating a win-win scenario that would fulfill their dreams while creating an expanding company. And most importantly, I learned and implemented a culture that made people feel valued, appreciated, and supported, which has continued to be the cornerstone of my work.

In 2003, I felt that I had accomplished and contributed all that I could in that role (I hope that you are also lovingly growing your teams out of a job!) and left to form HINGE Early Education Advisors. Putting the "s" on "Advisors" was a glimpse into the future I hoped to create, as it was only me for several years! Like many of you, I borrowed money and struggled for many years, traveling and working crazy hours and risking my family's financial well-being to try to make a bigger difference in the industry. Beginning in a consulting role relating to growth, I quickly realized that I could be more successful if I supported business owners in purchasing schools or selling their businesses and real estate. I found that the nearly twenty years of relationship-building I had invested in during my former work paid off in creating a strong buyer base for schools.

The path has not always been smooth. I have experienced a significant economic downturn where my work shut down for nearly two years, and in this field where we only get paid when sellers get paid, that meant zero income for those two years. Although I was prepared before the downturn with enough cash to survive the classic six months that financial advisors recommend, I borrowed money during this time to pay my bills and support my family, and invested heavily in creating more relationships that I hoped would lead to successful work when the economy strengthened. And the investment paid off! The next ten years saw steady growth, and I coached younger team members to prepare for a much longer gap in revenue. Years later I led the company through a global pandemic, expecting the same kind of challenges. As transaction work halted, we invested in bringing valuable information to the industry about how other providers were navigating challenging operations and financial viability, again drawing on many years of relationship building in asking many others to contribute. But this time, the gap was only months. The world took notice of the critical nature of the industry, with its sophisticated systems and adaptation to stay open so that essential workers could do their jobs. And the phone began ringing. . .

Today the HINGE team is located nationwide, serving clients all across the world, and I feel incredibly blessed to be in their presence. The beginning small buyer base has grown to over 500 groups wanting to expand or enter the industry, and the team I am so blessed to work with has, to date, gained over $1 billion in value for our clients. That is what keeps me moving forward: the idea that I can make a meaningful difference in the lives of early education business owners by helping them thrive personally, while creating stronger programs, *and* exiting when the time is right for them, and at a business and real estate value that they deserve for their future. In addition to our transaction services, we are serving owners with opportunities to help them thrive financially—in delivery systems that include conference and affiliate organization speaking engagements on business and financial topics, providing monthly informational webinars, offering our free Framework app to help business owners access their revenue and expense benchmark, supporting them with financial and coaching services and leadership training, and creating and delivering our annual signature in-house events such as THRIVE and SHIFT. It is all mind-blowing as I spell it out. But like many of you, when I see a meaningful opportunity that supports those I care about, I simply can't not do it!

As I have said many times, this industry that I love so dearly is stuck with me. They are going to have to bury me out back.

໑

Implementation Tips

Build relationships with others who share your vision and never compromise a relationship. Stay true to your mission no matter how others behave or what they choose to do. You can create more together than individually!

Don't underestimate the power of your story. Telling it often and with humility can create connections with staff, parents, and others in your community. Be curious about others and their thoughts. If faced with anger or defiance, ask what is driving that reaction in a sincere and caring way.

Chapter 2
No Money, No Mission—A Shifting Mindset

The concepts of money and mission—serving children and families in high quality settings while creating a financially thriving organization—are often perceived as at odds with each other. The perception is that if a service-based business owner thrives financially, it must be at the expense of the people they serve. This is especially true if the people they serve are vulnerable children and families. Actually, those two things not only *can* be accomplished at once, but they are *necessary* for each other's survival.

Money, or profit, should be thought of as one of the tools to accomplish a mission or a purpose, Profit is never a sustainable goal in itself. What is the profit for? It might be developed to create a stable work environment for your employees and to reward them for the work that they do. It might be to serve children and families in thriving educational environments, or it might be to grow your business to serve more families and to create new opportunities for your team. Without meaningful purpose, profit is an empty goal.

It is equally important that it is not possible for you, the business owner, to continue to give and risk, without securing and thriving in your personal financial position. A scenario where you fail to thrive personally is not sustainable and will show quickly in the lack of support that your many stakeholders receive. Better said, developing and operating a business that serves hundreds of children and families each day, creates thriving work environments for early education professionals, and supports the risk-taker who put it all on the line must absolutely thrive financially to achieve the mission it intends. Without profit, no worthwhile purpose is possible. The two must work and thrive together. It isn't possible also to *only* focus on giving.

Adding to the perception that thriving is not a worthy goal are the many articles that state (with implied horror) that early education now costs more than a college education. Good! It should!! Isn't it logical that we invest more in the expense associated with the care and education of our most vulnerable population? A population that is best served with a low staff to child ratio and in high quality environments versus a population that has some (hopefully!) measure of self sufficiency in environments with much higher staff to student ratios and with more financial resources that support the cost? Not withstanding the idea that birth to five is highly recognized as the most important stage of a human's development and critical to life long success.

While I am sometimes accused of being insensitive to the needs of working families, this is certainly not my intention. The high cost of quality early education has profound implications for families, especially those with lower incomes. For many, the cost of childcare can create a significant financial burden on top of the cost of food, shelter, and medical care. This can force parents to make difficult choices such as reducing work hours, giving up potential career advancement, and using informal and potentially less safe childcare arrangements that lack the essential development educational components all children deserve at the most important time in their development. And, as a professional who once depended on an early education system to work and survive, and now the parent of three young adults who have children of their own in childcare, I am intimately aware of the financial challenges that come from wanting the best care and education for vulnerable babies and young children. I want that for all children. I don't pretend to understand what global solutions are necessary to rectify the financial balance of early education for families and teachers. What I do know is that people who risk greatly must balance that risk with the ability to thrive. And you, my business owner, deserve an advocate too.

The caring and giving nature of the early education community is what has kept me in this industry since 1986. I could have used my accounting and growth skills in other places, and I could have helped business owners grow and sell their businesses and real estate in other industries. I lost count years ago of the number of incredible businesses that I have had the pleasure to support and transition and I have never, ever, in all of those years, had one single person, company, financial partner, landlord, or any stakeholder, interested in *only* making money. If I had, I imagine that they would be short-lived in this community. What keeps me locked in is the incredible people who have focused their lives on serving children, staff, and families.

And so my intention is to continue to be an advocate for you, the business owner. I'm going to advocate for you and your business because you cannot possibly do the mission you set out to do if you are not financially healthy. Should there be other answers and support systems? Yes! But until there are, you must continue to be your own advocate of financial health. And I will be right there with you.

Chapter 3

Benchmarking

A benchmark, by definition, is a standard or point of reference against which things may be compared or assessed. Early in my career as a financial manager, I was often frustrated by the lack of meaningful standards for revenue and expense assessment that would allow me to know if the schools I was supporting were doing well. In addition, coaching directors to make good decisions around tuition rates and other charges, as well as expense management, was a shot in the dark. I found out quickly that most financial and business concepts were confusing and difficult for our directors and our managers who were making fast decisions all day long. My mission became to help them compile and break down information in the simplest and most meaningful way, so that they could use it to do the critical work that they needed to do.

Although I had created a financial statement format that I felt was simple and would be understandable to decision-makers, it still lacked the validation of responsible revenue setting and expense control. But in 1990, an opportunity arose when several similar-sized companies agreed to share their financial statements. I must admit that it was one of my best days (sad, but true!) when I was able to spread the statements out over the large conference table and study the way their finances behaved.

What I found was fascinating and comforting. I found that early education companies that were financially stable managed their expenses and the percent of tuition they spent in each expense category in ways that were almost identical. And the early Framework model began. Because of today's work at HINGE, we are continually reviewing the financial performance of childcare companies small and large, single and multi-site, for-profit and non-profit, play-based and special-ity curriculums, in rural and urban markets, each and every day. And while in-dividual performance is confidential and never shared, the analysis allows us to monitor possible shifts in the market and changes in revenue and expense behavior. Since 1990, the model has only shifted slightly. The first change occurred in 2008 with marketing expenses decreasing (does anyone remember yellow pages?) and employee benefits increasing as the industry began its challenges in hiring excellent team members, with the two changes nearly offsetting each other.

We saw a stabilization of the financial model for many years, followed by the vol-atility of changing expense structures in wages following the COVID-19 pandemic years, when spending for staff, supplies, and safety protocols skyrocketed and the loss of revenue was offset by federal and state grant funding. Now that grant funding has largely been eliminated and costs are settling, emerging trends seem to have morphed into current normal protocols, and we are monitoring several, such as increased payment processing fees, increased staff costs, and increased insurance costs. However, these trends will need to normalize across the majority of schools and stabilize over time before we will consider adjusting the model. I hope that as you get to know the model you find its stability as comforting as I do, because even though strategies to reach the benchmarks change, the benchmarks themselves are incredibly stable and can be a powerful part of a planning and tracking process.

As you read and consider this information, I invite you to go to Framework-byHinge.com and choose "Free Assessment." Input your school's billing cycle (weekly or monthly), licensed capacity and average tuition rate (for most schools the full-time three-year-old rate), and current occupancy. The application will populate to show you what the average financially healthy school, given your size and tuition rate structure, at your current occupancy, will spend in each expense category. The first set of columns will give you a current benchmark, and you can use the drop-down tabs to expand each expense section. The second set of columns will allow you to adjust your benchmark at different occupancy levels. This exercise will be most helpful as we go through the Five Pillars in subsequent chapters.

Today there are thousands of companies that have used and continue to use the Framework benchmark. Many business owners have elected to use the format in Framework to produce their own financial statements more effectively, using the model for comparison. Think of the benchmark as a powerful point of reference that allows you to measure your financial performance against industry standards and peer performance. Use them as aspirational targets, setting your sights on out-performing industry averages. This pursuit of excellence isn't just about financial gain, but about creating an environment that sets your early education business apart in terms of quality and impact. Financial benchmarks act as a spotlight, revealing hidden corners of your business that may otherwise go unnoticed. By comparing your performance to industry averages, you can identify areas where improvement is needed, ensuring that no financial blind spots jeopardize your business success. Benchmarks aren't just about surviving—they're about thriving.

❦

Implementation Tips

Make benchmarking a collaborative endeavor within your team and foster a culture that values continuous improvement, where everyone understands the importance of benchmarking in driving operational success. Encourage open dialogue about the targets and how they contribute to the shared vision of the team. Help the team understand how a full, thriving school contributes to your ability to support their jobs, pay, benefits, curriculum and materials, and a top-quality facility.

Help parent customers understand the economics of how the average school spends their tuition dollars and how you are good stewards of their valuable resources. Use the model outlined in Chapter 13 as a communication guide.

Support local, state, and national efforts to educate legislators on the economic model of early education companies and where support and oversight is best spent.

Part II

The Five Pillars

Introduction to the Five Pillars

For many years, seeing the glassy-eyed stare of owners and directors when (or if!) they received their school's financial statement, I felt that there must be a simpler way to orient them to an understanding of the relevance of the data, along with actionable steps to align with healthy standards. At the core of the data are five key controllable areas that, if prioritized, will move the school toward greater financial health. These five items are simple to understand and strategize. So instead of focusing on ninety-nine different things, focusing on the five key areas makes the analysis easier and gives decision-makers a greater sense of control.

Driving Revenue

The first three Pillars—occupancy, tuition rates, and discounts—all relate to driving the revenue that a school has to support the healthy expense load necessary to create quality. A sufficient amount of revenue is required just to cover basic fixed expenses (rent or mortgage, utilities, insurance, property taxes, management, and key staff). An abundance of revenue is required to then create a thriving school that is able to support experienced and qualified team members, curriculum, materials, and supplies for a dynamic experience, and a physical environment conducive to care and learning. The first three pillars work together to create the primary revenue source a school utilizes to operate. You will never "expense control" your way to financial health. Without a stable and thriving revenue base, the school will always struggle.

Expense Control

Pillars Four and Five are the largest expenses involved in operating a typical early education program: staff salaries and rent or mortgage. Understanding and managing a healthy target ratio between these expenses and revenue is critical for the school's success.

Of the Five Pillars, there are two that need to be managed and thought about every day: occupancy and staff costs. The three others can be managed, at most, a couple of times a year, and at least once a year: tuition rates, discounts, and facility costs. I invite you to consider each individually as we explore these concepts in greater detail.

Meet Harriet

Harriet Had a Dream

Harriet had an amazing career as a university level French teacher. She valued education and studied hard to reach a high level of achievement in her career. Her passion was for students to understand the value in their education and gain exposure to different languages and cultures. When her first child was born, she took a modest maternity leave and then began looking for a high-quality learning environment for her young daughter while she worked. Although she found some options in her community that she felt would be safe and caring, she was disappointed with the options that supported her dream of having her children exposed to a diverse group of children and cultures, in stimulating environments, with a modern facility and high-quality classroom materials. Harriet decided that to provide all that she wanted for her daughter, she would need to create it herself! After all, she was an educator.

Harriet Developed Her Company

Harriet searched for meaningful business help as she was launching her company and found some useful resources in her local small business development group and a local real estate broker. She became frustrated though that no one seemed to be able to tell her how to open an early education business and how to operate it efficiently. With big dreams, some personal savings, and a small loan from her parents, she found a building to rent and convinced the landlord to invest in the interior space and playground. Along with her personal funds and loan from her parents, Harriet took out a small SBA loan to supplement the cost of equipment, furniture, and curriculum and cover any start-up losses. She began to feel nervous that the secure level of income she had worked so hard to achieve in teaching was gone and that everything she had, including her family's well-being, was now at risk. She developed the curriculum herself, supplementing it with some early education resources focused on teaching foreign language and introducing the students to diverse cultures. Harriet took a look at local childcare centers and set her tuition rates a bit lower, wanting to attract families quickly. She decided to offer discounts to her team for their own childcare costs and to families who were absent for illness or vacation. Her local competitors didn't give a discount to families if they had more than one child enrolled in the school, so she decided not to do that either. Harriet wanted to hire the best teachers and knew that she would need to pay more than her competition in order to attract quality talent. After the extensive and exhausting processes of permitting, renovations, and licensing, Harriet was ready for business!

Harriet Opened the Doors

The first year was a big challenge, but Harriet expected that. She found herself in a continual process of hiring, training, opening new classes, and juggling parent communication and staff performance issues. Harriet felt that she was falling behind in meeting parent demands and behavorial issues in the classrooms, and she was working from opening to closing, putting a strain on her family. She knew that she should hire a director at some point, but with her cash still not at a breakeven point, she didn't want to commit to a large salary for a director. She found herself covering classes regularly when teachers were sick. She felt that her enrollment was strong, but she was still struggling financially. Harriet wondered what she was doing wrong.

Harriet's First Two Years

For the first year, Harriet had to go back to her parents for a second loan because she was not cash positive and found herself in a difficult Catch-22. She was working twelve-hour days to help support teachers and cover classrooms and didn't have enough information to understand why she was still struggling. She wasn't even sure if she was collecting all of the money that was due. Harriet was exhausted every day after work and waking in the middle of the night concerned about making payroll and the rent. By the beginning of the second year, Harriet attended a state childcare conference and heard Kathy Ligon of HINGE Advisors speak about the Five Pillars of Purpose-Driven Profit. Her initial reaction was that this person's advice was probably not sound, because she said not to worry about salaries and rent until the school had a healthy level of occupancy. What?! Don't worry about expenses? Well, the advice was not exactly "don't worry," but do your best and then focus on enrolling. And though Kathy's ideas sounded questionable, she WAS old and HAD been around the industry for a long time. Harriet did know that she couldn't keep up this pace much longer. Her family was suffering and so was she. Harriet needed something different. So she began year two with a mission to work on her business—not in it!

Chapter 4

Pillar One—Occupancy

Go no further until this chapter is mastered! Occupancy, simply, is the percentage of available spaces filled by enrolled children. It is the most critical Pillar and a major metric for the success and sustainability of early education centers. Occupancy directly impacts the center's financial health, quality of care, and ability to serve the community. Without a healthy number of children paying tuition, the school's fixed costs such as management and lead teaching teams, rent, property taxes, insurance, and basic supplies cannot be covered.

Most schools, if modelled correctly with tuition rates that match the cost of care and rent or mortgage costs that are in line with healthy benchmarks (see Pillars two and five), will produce a breakeven point at 50-60% occupancy, and will be able to begin to approach financial health at 70-75% full. Recall that financial health is defined as the ability to earn enough revenue to hire staff at healthy wages and support their training, retention, and benefits needs; maintain regulatory compliance; invest in high quality curriculum and supplies; develop and maintain safe and inviting facilities and learning spaces; create resources to reinvest in and grow the company; and support the owner with personal resources—all working together to create a thriving environment for the many stakeholders that the business supports. Once the school begins to operate in occupancy ranges of

75-100%, fixed costs should be covered, and resources should become abundant as additional tuition at this level will cover possible assistant-level teachers and extra food and supplies. The majority of this revenue will flow to the bottom line, developing the resources necessary to reinvest and grow the business. Maintaining enrollment at this level is vital for the financial health required to create the important work that you set out to do.

If your school is not at least 70% full to licensed capacity, you will never thrive, so if that's not the case, your primary focus is on enrollment building in the school. In 2024, we are in a high demand market since unemployment is low. Parents are working and have an increased awareness of, and are investing more in, the positive effects of high-quality group learning environments. The trade-off in this economic environment is difficulty in hiring, as competition for staff is high. During other economic times, unemployment is high, and enrollments are a struggle, but hiring is less difficult. After experiencing both cycles many times, I personally prefer a high-demand environment where enrollments are less challenging. We can implement strategies to hire, retain, and develop teams (more on that in Pillar Four), but we have limited ability to influence parent decisions when they are not working.

There are three basic methods for calculating occupancy, each with increasing complexity, but also with increasing accuracy and information that allows for healthy decision making. All three methods are calculated by comparing some metric to the licensed capacity. I encourage the majority of business owners to use the actual licensed capacity and not their own internal "effective capacity"— meaning the number they have decided is their maximum capacity. The reason for that is that you could, in fact, enroll to licensed capacity. You might have a good reason not to, such as group sizes when it is not cost effective to hire another teacher to add one or two enrollments to a classroom, or you feel that your level of quality isn't conducive to higher ratios, but it is important to have the information that shows you the impact of your decisions. This is not to say that your decisions are wrong, but that they are intentional decisions that impact the financial picture in your school. So, for our calculations, let's use actual licensed capacity.

After learning more about the Five Pillars, Harriet decided that she didn't have much to lose in making some changes in her business practices, because the cash drain could not continue. She decided to dig in and follow the best practices she had learned toward financial health. Initially Harriet believed that her school was well-enrolled, since she had all of her classes open. But now, learning more about the impact of occupancy on her financial health, she thought differently about the additional space she had in each classroom for one or two new enrollments. To support that, she recently started a waitlist—one that she felt she could depend on as parents had paid deposits to secure their child's spot.

Her original fear in maximizing her ratios was that the team would be too stressed if she added more children. Contributing to her fear was that she had lost two teachers to out-of-industry positions that were less stressful, which made her nervous about adding more students. She went back and forth with questions in her mind. How much of an impact would a couple of students make? Was she going to stress teachers even more? At the same time, she knew that what she was doing was not sustainable in the long run, no matter how great her intentions were.

To mitigate that risk, she decided to involve the entire staff in a conversation about what a stronger enrollment would mean to the school in the form of increased pay and benefits, as well as abundant classroom resources and advancement opportunities for the team. In addition, she worked with the team on how they could participate in enrollment by developing prospective parent tours that pointed out the unique features of the school and focused on customer service and parent engagement.

At the end of the day, Harriet was determined to make her dream a thriving business. She began working on the Five Pillars by focusing on occupancy first.

Method 1. The Headcount Method

A simple headcount method is fast and easy. In this method, the number of students enrolled is compared to the licensed capacity.

For instance, Harriet's school is licensed for 110 students, and there are 92 students enrolled. In her example, she will divide the currently enrolled students (92) into the licensed capacity (110). The result with this method is that the school is 83.64% full (92/100 = .8364).

Calculation

92 enrolled students / 110 licensed capacity = .8364 or 83.64% occupancy

---

This calculation says that of all the children Harriet could potentially serve in this building, she is serving 83.64% of that number. There are several hidden dangers in using this method alone, but it can also be a quick gauge of increases and decreases in enrollment.

Method 2. The FTE Method

FTE, or Full-Time Equivalent, is a common method used to more accurately calculate occupancy, adding full-time and part-time enrollments into measurable full-time units. In this method, full-time students are counted as 1 enrollment, and part-time students are counted as ½ enrollment. In this method, FTE, instead of headcount, is compared to the licensed capacity.

Using the same information for Harriet above, of the 92 enrolled children, 70 are full-time and 22 are part-time. Full-time students are counted as 1 (70 full-time) and part-time students are counted as ½ (22 part-time x ½ = 11). Adding the full-time of 70 to the part-time of 11, we get an FTE of 88. We then compare the FTE of 88 to the licensed capacity of 110, and the school is 80% full (88/110 = .8).

Calculation

88 FTE / 110 licensed capacity = .8 or 80% occupancy

This more detailed information says logically that there is greater capacity to enroll than Harriet thought under the headcount method as she has now considered the effect of part-time students. Before and after school populations are counted as part-time (except in holiday or summer periods) and there are times when enrollment-building means that you can be more flexible with part-time programming. Part-time students are not a bad decision and are particularly useful when ramping up a new or under-performing school. But when approaching maximum capacity, it is healthier to either request that part-time students begin full-time schedules, or to combine part-time programs that then equal full-time attendance (for instance, requiring either two-day and three-day schedules that combine for a full week and setting these at a higher tuition than one full-time student). Note also that in this challenging hiring environment, part-time programs can potentially be more difficult for teachers to manage.

Accuracy increased using the FTE method by showing that Harriet's occupancy was actually 3.64 children lower than the headcount method indicated, pointing out a greater ability to enroll. Harriet was now more aware of her ability to enroll and ready to focus her time and marketing efforts toward filling those slots. She was beginning to understand the value of 3-4 more children in her program and in including her team in the strategy and helping them to grow as professionals.

Method 3. The Revenue Maximization Method

The most informative method, and one that considers all aspects of the revenue picture including tuition rates, other charges such as registration fees and late payment fees, and the effects of discounting, is what i refer to as the revenue maximization method. Simply, this method is based on what cash actually is available to meet expense obligations. At the end of the day, that is what matters the most in maintaining financial health. This method will arm you with the information you need to consider the impact of the tuition rate and discounting decisions you are making and how they impact your ability to operate. There could be hidden dangers in the more basic methods that are not uncovered using headcount and FTE methods.

In Harriet's business, the school earns $1,200,000 in net revenue annually. Net revenue is the cash available to go in the bank for paying expenses—i.e. tuition income plus other charges, minus discounts. This amount can be found easily on the Income line of your tax return, or from your billing system—typically in some version of an annual Total Charge Credit Summary report. In our example, the school earns $1,270,000 in annual tuition income, $10,000 in other charges (initial registration fees, late payment fees, etc.) and discounts $80,000 (see Pillar Three).

Calculation
$1,270,000 tuition income + $10,000 other charges - $80,000 discounts = $1,200,000 net revenue

Further, in Harriet's school, the average tuition rate weekly is $310. The average tuition rate for a school that serves infant through afterschool populations will typically be the three-year-old tuition rate, as infant/toddler tuition rates are usually higher, and afterschool tuition rates are typically lower. Our licensed capacity is 110.

Calculation

$1,200,000 annual net revenue / 110 licensed capacity / $310 average weekly tuition rate / 52 weeks = .6767 or 67.67% occupancy

What this says is that of all the revenue that Harriet could earn using this facility without changing the tuition rate or licensed capacity, she is earning 67.67% of that. Using the revenue maximization method uncovered some possibilities for bringing the school into greater financial health and has revealed less than minimum financial health occupancy of 70%. At a revenue maximization occupancy of 67.67%, the school is missing some opportunities for stability. Some additional strategies might be to consider whether the tuition rates are actually covering the cost of services (see Pillar Two), or whether there is the opportunity to increase other income (see notes on other income), or if discounts can be eliminated or reduced (see Pillar Three).

But Harriet learned to focus on occupancy first, so she now decides to take a risk and hire a director that in the short run will put her financial health at greater risk, but in the long run will allow her to focus on enrollment building and supporting the staff to prepare for more students.

The investment paid off! After a few months, Harriet managed to enroll to 80% capacity by adding thirteen additional students. Without changing the tuition rate, she now earns $1,418,500 in net revenue annually, an increase of $218,560! Harriet is starting to feel more confident in her ability to free herself up to strategize healthy business practices and implement them in a healthy way.

Calculation

$1,418,560 annual net revenue / 110 licensed capacity / $310 average weekly tuition rate / 52 weeks = .8 or 80% occupancy

With the new enrollment, Harriet is maximizing the ability of the school to serve more families, while creating greater financial resources to hire, add pay and benefits, and possibly grow to serve even more families. She quickly realized that the new enrollments were in classes where costs were already covered, making the majority of the revenue gained—except for a bit more food and supplies—complete profit! This one change meant that she was now financially stable after hiring her director. With the excess cash, she could dream of adding a new supplemental curriculum and hiring a floater to alleviate teacher burnout.

Closely tracking occupancy is critical to the success of your childcare business and the well-being of families and teams. Knowing the impact of your enrollment decisions on the overall financial picture is vital.

∾

Implementation Tips

Closely monitor occupancy at a minimum each week, if not each day. Know where your ability to enroll is and create marketing strategies to gain the last one or two students in each classroom. Consider moving classes in the building based on demand and maximizing group sizes.

If occupancy is 70% or above and you are not able to align with the Framework percentages, then consider whether your tuition rates are sufficiently covering the cost of service you are providing (see Pillar Two). If occupancy is under 70%, focus on enrollment strategies. If occupancy is between 70-90%, then also focus on occupancy strategies until you reach the healthiest possible occupancy of 90% and above.

If you have a much higher FTE percent and a much lower revenue maximization percent, you're probably discounting too much or not charging the actual cost of care.

If you are making choices to increase quality by reducing ratios—great! Just be sure and charge the tuition rate that reflects that level of quality and cost of care, and you can still maximize revenue.

Once you know your occupancy, use the Framework App by selecting your current occupancy to see what your expenses should be. If you are having difficulty aligning with the benchmark and your occupancy is healthy, do a thorough analysis of Pillars Two and Three, tuition rates and discounts.

Explain the value of maximizing occupancy to the team (see Chapter 13). Once they understand the value of full classrooms on your ability to pay them more, provide benefits and training and opportunities for individual growth—one more child in their classroom feels a bit better! Further, bonusing the team for their part in enrolling and retaining enrollment creates an environment of joint success!

Build a relationship with other stakeholders in your community; include Early Head Start and Head Start providers and the local school district. As other organizations have funding available for early childhood programs, be a part of the solution. Be a program that is recognized as quality learning and the first partner thought of when new programs are funded and implemented. Relationships are key when others make decisions about expanding programs and partnering with their resources. Don't be left behind while competing programs are funded.

Consider bidding for the afterschool program at your local elementary schools. Distinguish yourself as an educational provider and focus on supplemental learning like foreign language, culture education, values education, etc.

Chapter 5
Pillar Two—Tuition Rates

Buckle up for some *big* thoughts on this one! Setting tuition rates that reflect the cost of services is one of the most difficult tasks for an early education business owner. There is a delicate balance between what it costs to create quality learning environments and the ability of families or subsidy support systems to pay. When setting tuition rates, it is essential to consider the cost of care along with the economic circumstances of the community the center serves. Pricing should be affordable for families while also ensuring that the center can maintain quality services and meet its financial obligations.

Historically, many childcare business owners have determined tuition rates by asking their competitors what they charge and developing a strategy to be slightly under or slightly over that rate. There are several critical issues with taking this approach. The first issue is considering whether those you are polling are true competitors. Someone providing childcare in your market is not necessarily a competitor. A competitor is someone providing services in your market, with the same level of programming, curriculum, and staff quality, in a facility with similar quality and the same offerings such as hours and age groups served. The second issue is that those operators you are polling might not be charging the cost of care and could be living in fear of the result of increasing tuition rates. It is possible that you may need to be the trend setter in your current market, or in a new market, to provide higher quality and set a new bar for the expectation of tuition rates. Your rates should reflect the unique value proposition of your school.

Cost of Care

What does cost of care mean? The cost of care refers to the total expenses involved in providing care and education to children at your early education center. Unlike market-based pricing, which primarily looks at what other centers charge, the cost of care approach is grounded in your specific operational costs. This ensures that your tuition rates reflect the actual expenses of running your center, allowing you to maintain quality and financial health. In other words, it is necessary to take a "backwards" approach. Instead of blindly following the local crowd, you should, instead, determine your particular expenses coupled with your business goals, and then determine the appropriate rate to match.

Operating a business in the early education industry requires a heavy expense load, making it difficult to balance tuition rates with parent affordability. In a typical school with a normalized occupancy of 70% and above (disregarding the sharp staff increases currently being experienced that are making the traditional model challenging for most providers), operating costs include the following, based on a percentage of all tuition dollars paid:

- Staff costs such as salaries, payroll taxes, benefits, and recruiting and training at about 50-55%
- Program costs such as food, supplies, advertising, vehicles, and dues and licenses at approximately 12-15%
- Facility costs such as rent or mortgage, repairs and maintenance, janitorial, security, insurance, property taxes, utilities, averaging 22-25%
- Administrative costs such as bank and ACH or credit card fees, billing systems, office supplies, travel, and internet at around 3-5%.

This cost structure, at 70% occupancy, equates to 90% to 100% of all tuition dollars paid, leaving no resources for capital repairs, improvements, and growth. At lower occupancies, the school is likely losing cash, which is not a sustainable model. And at higher occupancies, it is possible to begin to gain the resources for reinvestment in the company and growth. With a heavy cost structure business there are slim margins, and balancing tuition rates with the cost of care is critical.

Price Communicates Quality

In addition to covering the cost of care, the tuition rate isn't just a number, but a statement. It communicates not only the cost of services but also the perceived quality and value that an early education center offers. When tuition rates are "less than," all the consumer hears is "less than." And in the absence of a clear understanding of quality and what that means, consumers often use price as a gauge for quality.

Consider this analogy: I want to buy a bottle of wine for a special occasion, but I don't know anything about wine. In an effort to be sure I am most likely purchasing something that is high quality, instead of going to the local supermarket, I go to a specialized wine store, believing that there is a team there who can support my decision. I feel good if the wine store is in a nice, well-maintained facility as it communicates that there is attention to detail. I ask to be led to a section where there is high-quality wine and I begin to ask the salesperson questions about my specific needs and desires. As I consider the options, knowing there is a limit to what I can afford, I am more inclined to a purchase with a bottle with a higher price, but not the highest, because I feel that the quality is probably higher than a lower priced purchase.

Of course, when I get home and enjoy the bottle of wine, if the quality is not what I perceived by speaking with a specialized team and experiencing it myself, I will stop going to that wine store. In other words, don't set yourself up for a "less than" perception from the market if you are truly a premium provider. It is never a good strategy.

Pricing Limits and Subsidy Support

I must strongly address the amount of respect we should all have for families with limited income, who have no other option than to secure their children's early education based on price. I have been that parent myself. There was a time as a young parent when paying the $45 per week tuition for my daughter was a stretch, even being a recent university graduate in a professional position. During that time, I also went to the grocery with a calculator since my weekly budget for food, diapers, formula, etc., was also $45 per week, and when the calculator indicated I was at the limit, the purchasing stopped! Until there is more support from outside sources (government, business, etc.) to supplement families who have limited fixed incomes, this challenge will remain, and families will be forced to limit their investment in high-quality early education. I certainly understand the difficulty in wanting more for my children and not having the resources to provide it.

Some families are eligible for and fortunate enough to receive the limited support available for childcare costs. Subsidy tuition (or tuition paid by a non-family source such as a government agency) is generally limited. A few states currently contribute the actual cost of care but most do not. Some states allow a contributing fee charged to parents to bridge the gap between the subsidy rate and the market rate, but owners often choose not to charge it, because they perceive that families can't afford it or their competitors don't charge the difference, making competition challenging. This creates a difficult balance between revenue and the cost of care.

There are currently initiatives in place in many states to use a cost of care model instead of a current tuition rate survey for setting tuition rates, and there is some discussion of increasing reimbursement rates to limit parent co-pays to a certain percentage of their income. Both initiatives could create a better financial environment for the families eligible for subsidy support and for the school, allowing more early education businesses to serve this community. In addition, there are initiatives to pay subsidy tuition on time, and base subsidies on enrollment instead of attendance. All of these possibilities should create a stronger ability to serve this population in high quality settings. Hopefully we can continue to partner with and educate those making decisions around the need for and cost of high-quality education and care.

Private pay tuition (or tuition paid directly by the consumer) offers more flexibility in balancing costs, though the ability of parents to pay is a necessary consideration.

Strategies for Tuition Rate Setting

Balancing Age Groups

For most schools, varying age groups pay different tuition rates because they cost different amounts to operate. Infant and toddler programs cost the most to operate as the staff-to-child ratios are much lower, and in a business where historically 50-55% of all tuition dollars support staff expenses, staff-to-child ratios are a key to price setting. For many schools, serving infants and toddlers is a loss leader—a service sold at a price that is not profitable but serves to attract new customers or sell additional services to those customers. In early education businesses, most schools will retain the younger children throughout the life of their preschool years and encourage the enrollment of siblings in older age groups. Preschool teacher-to-child ratios align more closely to cost of care, and afterschool care rates are typically lower than preschool rates during the school year, since this class group attends fewer hours per day.

When and How Much to Raise Rates

Most healthy schools will set a precedent of increasing tuition rates annually, at least to cover inflation. In times of increasing cost structures such as salaries and supplies, or in times of increasing regulation such as changing staff-to-child ratios or minimum wage increases, larger tuition rate increases or multiple tuition rate increases per year are necessary. On average, adjustments for typical inflation are 3-5% annually, but there have been increases of 8-12% in recent years and sometimes more than once a year. With pay rates reportedly increasing 30-50% since COVID-19 (see Pillar Four), even these sharp increases leave a gap in balancing staff costs at a healthy percentage of tuition paid.

Most schools will adjust rates at the beginning of the school year or at the beginning of the calendar year, but, in general, there is no particular time that works better than others. The key is to communicate well to parents with appreciation for their business and an explanation of the changes, along with a reasonable amount of time for them to prepare and consider other options for care if necessary.

At the present time, waitlists for enrollment are typical and are heavy in infant age groups. Some providers have used this high-demand period to more closely align infant tuition rates with the actual cost of care in an attempt to move more toward a breakeven cost-to-revenue model in those age groups. In general, when demand is strong enough to necessitate a waitlist, that is a good time to consider whether there is room to increase the tuition rate.

Determine Future Goals

Setting tuition rates is not just about covering current expenses but also about strategically positioning the center for future growth and sustainability. By carefully considering future goals, owners can also set tuition rates that support their long-term vision. Typical annual budgeting includes beginning with the prior year's performance, making adjustments based on goals for the coming year, and ending with a plan going forward.

In setting a budget, consider the following:

1. **Revenue Forecasting**
   a. Can you increase occupancy to make the cost percentage easier to manage?
   b. Do you plan to expand your school to accommodate more children or offer additional services?
   c. What tuition rate changes will you implement to ensure that they are sufficient to cover your projected future costs while maintaining a reasonable profit margin?
   d. Are you aiming to enhance the quality of your programs, such as by hiring new staff, increasing pay or benefits, adding a new curriculum component, or upgrading your facility or playgrounds?

2. **Expense Forecasting**
   a. How will you invest in ongoing training and development for your staff to enhance the quality of care and education provided?
   b. Are there expense items that you can manage more closely?

3. **Invest in Your School's Future**
   a. Do you want to build sufficient cash reserves to support the company through difficult times?
   b. Do you want to consider expanding into a second (or third, or additional) location to serve more of your community or in additional communities?
   c. Do you want to create growth and advancement opportunities for your team?

Catching Up

Once you have established a pattern of limiting tuition rates, it can be challenging to raise rates in the future. Families may become accustomed to lower rates and resist attempts to increase them, making it difficult to attain and maintain financial sustainability. If you have fallen behind on charging the actual cost of care, there are some viable strategies for catching up without stressing families too much at once.

One option is to grandfather current families in with a smaller rate increase and deem them "legacy families," thanking them for their loyalty and explaining what you are doing for them. A possible option is to use this strategy but not decrease the rate as the child ages into less expensive programs. At the same time, begin charging the cost of care rate to incoming families who can make the decision initially whether the rate works within their budgets.

In all grandfathering strategies, it is important to record the current tuition rate that is charged for new families in your billing system and apply a discount such as a legacy discount as an offset. This information can then be used to quantify the effect of your pricing decision and will also show the families the full effect of the concession you are making on their behalf.

Another option is to combine a smaller tuition rate increase with the addition of other fees such as annual registration, supply, or assessment charges, or with the elimination of a discount (see Pillar Three).

Communicating with Parents

All tuition rate increases should come with a kind explanation to parents as to why the increase is healthy and necessary. Educating parents about rising operating costs and increasing costs of hiring, retaining, and educating staff, along with your future goals to improve the school, is vital for their support in your business development. Parents are generally supportive of increases relating to care for their child and their child's teacher. A letter explaining the necessity of the increase and what it will be used for is a critical component of getting parent support. As hard as it is, unfortunately you might lose a family or two when you pass their pricing tolerance, but this may be necessary for the good of the school. You are not helping anyone if you put the company in jeopardy and lack the resources necessary to support the program, your team, and yourself.

Clearly communicate the value that parents and children will receive from your early education center, both now and in the future. Be transparent about your future goals and how your tuition rates support them, how your tuition rates are determined, and what they include. This builds trust with parents and helps them understand the value they are receiving. Establish a feedback loop with parents to understand their needs and preferences, allowing you to adapt your offerings and pricing accordingly. Maintain an open dialogue with parents to understand their perceptions of quality and value. Use this feedback to make adjustments to your services as needed.

Collecting Your Money

While charging the right amount for the services you provide is critical, collecting the tuition you have earned is even more critical! Income collection is an important aspect of managing an early education center's finances. Timely and efficient collection of fees from parents is essential for maintaining financial stability, providing quality care, and ensuring the long-term success of the company. Timely income collection ensures a steady cash flow, which is vital for meeting operating expenses such as staff salaries, rent, and utilities. Knowing how much income to expect and when to expect it will allow you to create accurate budgets and financial plans for future growth and development. No amount of planning and strategizing will be sufficient without collecting the money for services you provide! In addition, collecting income in a systematic way enables the company to maintain accurate financial records, which is essential for reporting, analysis, and decision-making.

Over the years, as early education business owners and managers have proudly recognized the value of their work, collecting money has become less of an issue. The elimination or reduction of accepting cash and check payments for the majority of the industry and the increased use of automatic payment systems have also contributed to lessening this challenge. Note that some parent groups have difficulty using automatic payment systems and continue to rely on check and cash, necessitating greater attention to collecting payments.

At the end of the day, it is unfair to those showing up to work at your school every day to not be compensated for their labor. It is also not helpful to families to allow them to fall so far behind on making payments that they are not able to catch up. Use a system to access overdue payments weekly and, except in emergency situations, and with long-term families, do not compromise on your collection policy. Most schools charge tuition in advance of services and impose a late payment fee when the tuition is late. Make a practice of charging the fee immediately to encourage on-time payments and avoid stress on the school's cashflow. Consistently enforce late fees and have a clear policy for disenrollment if payments are not made. Trends toward more efficient collection of tuition are beneficial and vital for your school's health, reducing the administrative burden on staff and allowing them to focus on providing quality care. Whenever possible, move toward monthly tuition rates along with automatic billing and payment collection systems.

As Harriet recently conducted a hiring process, she noticed that pay rates were increasing. New team members were demanding higher wages, and she was losing candidates to higher paying jobs in other industries. With the increased wages, Harriet was now spending more for salaries and wondered if she was not managing her staff hours well. She considered whether she was still charging the cost of care tuition rate, as she knew that issues balancing staff spending percentages could be less about too many hours and more about not charging enough to cover her costs. Her new dreams of training her teachers in new classroom management techniques, investing in a new curriculum enhancement program, and seeking an accreditation seemed out of reach as she began to, once again, conserve cash. Harriet was successful with Pillar One and felt more confident to now consider her tuition rates.

As a reminder, Harriet's financial picture looked like this after increasing occupancy to 80%.

Calculation

$1,418,560 annual net revenue / 110 licensed capacity / $310 average weekly tuition rate / 52 weeks = .8 or 80% occupancy

What does all this mean? Of all the revenue Harriet could earn in this building, given the current average tuition rate, she is earning 80% of that amount. Harriet also knew that at this level of revenue maximization occupancy, she should have abundant resources to invest in her school.

Harriet wondered if her original strategy to keep her tuition rates slightly lower than the local competition was actually working against her. Perhaps she was not getting credit within the community as a high-quality program, and perhaps her tuition rates weren't sufficient to cover the new cost of care with recent rising staffing costs. She had seen an increase in staff salaries of 35% recently, and with the help of the Framework benchmarking tool, she calculated that she needed to increase tuition rates by 12%. Harriet considered a smaller increase to not burden her families, but knew that she couldn't effectively support her teachers and cover other necessary costs to ensure that her students would thrive without bold action. Although this new tuition rate would put her a bit above other local operators, she knew that her high-quality program was superior and that her team was the best. She decided, nervously, to implement the change and hope for the best. The 12% increase would move the average tuition from $310 to $347 weekly. Harriet calculated that if she lost no enrollment, then her new financial picture would look like this:

Calculation
110 licensed capacity * $347 average weekly tuition rate * 52 weeks* 80% occupancy = $1,587,872 annual net revenue

By increasing the tuition rate for current families by 12%, Harriet would increase her annual net revenue by $169,312. This cash increase could go a long way to hire additional staff, increase pay or benefits, improve the curriculum or facility, or grow to serve more children.

Another interesting calculation Harriet considered before making the change in her tuition rates was to forecast how many enrollments could be lost and not lose revenue. In our example, the answer was 9.

Calculation
$169,312 increase in annual net revenue / $347 weekly average tuition rate / 52 weeks = 9.38

Once she decided to implement the tuition rate increase, Harriet was sad to lose a family with two children to a lower-cost option. Although she didn't want to put a strain on anyone, she understood the value in the tough decision to align her tuition rates with the actual cost of care necessary to create a thriving school. She also saw how hard her team worked every day and their passion for teaching and growing to serve more children in new and creative ways. Her current waitlist meant that she quickly enrolled two new students and was happy with her decision!

The accurate setting of the tuition rate of an early education center is a powerful tool for creating the type of school and services you intend, along with communicating quality and value to parents. By setting rates that align with the quality of your services, being transparent in your communication, and staying attuned to market dynamics, you can ensure that your pricing strategy effectively reflects and enhances the excellence of your school.

Historically, many early education business owners have lived in fear of losing enrollment with higher tuition rates or have put the needs of families over the needs of the school and their own personal need to thrive. As much as this is a noble cause, it is not sustainable. It does not work. You will never create the necessary resources to treat your dedicated and hard-working team well if you don't have the tuition rate set at a cost of care rate. You will never be able to create or continue to provide the high-quality education that children deserve. You will never be personally stable and financially and emotionally strong and you will not be able to continue to give. Living in fear of increasing tuition rates will never serve anyone well. Tuition rates must be set at the cost of care to succeed.

Recognize and don't discount your worth as an early education professional. If you are an owner who has held rates artificially lower than your school can support, you are not alone. However, your delay in increasing rates will begin to impact your ability to provide strong educational programs, build quality staff and curriculum, invest in facility needs, provide salary increases to deserving staff, and take care of other financial obligations. Don't sacrifice yourself and your financial well-being. After all, how can you possibly support the staff, parents, and children in your care if you are awake at night worried about making payroll and the mortgage?

Again, my wish is for all families to be able to afford the cost of care tuition rate, or if not, that they can gain the support they need to make that investment for their children. Until that happens, though, you must make decisions for the collective health of your school and team.

ᶜ∕ᵌ
Implementation Tips

Use the Framework app to "test" tuition rates given your licensed capacity and with varying occupancy levels. At 70% occupancy, a school should be able to achieve a 15% net income with the appropriate tuition rates. Remember that the net income does not include capital improvement and growth, which is where the necessity for a healthy net income lies. You can do this manually using the Free Assessment or use the paid version to test the results of increases at certain dollar amounts and percentages.

Calculate the number of FTEs that can be lost and maintain the same level of Net Revenue following a tuition rate increase. Over time this information will allow you to track how many are actually lost and will indicate the market tolerance of your increases.

Review cost of care and tuition rates quarterly in times of quick enrollment changes or cost shifts and implement changes to rates as needed.

Consider whether discounting tuition as a way to enroll new families could potentially damage your brand.

Whenever possible, move toward monthly tuition rates along with automatic billing and collection systems.

Inform parents at least a month in advance of any changes and explain the reasons for the changes.

Educate parents and other decision-makers on the cost of care (see Chapter 13).

If you are in danger of losing your business and are underwater in terms of your cost of care compared with what parents and caregivers are paying, then adjusting the tuition rates quickly to the cost of care is necessary. Doing this might cause you to lose some families, but it is better to lose a few families than to lose the ability to serve anyone and to have to terminate your team and disrupt children.

Chapter 6

Pillar Three—Discounts

Hidden danger, hidden danger! Managing decisions around discounting tuition is an area of opportunity for creating stronger financial health. As in managing occupancy, discounting is not bad, and there are some necessary applications for discounting. Also similar to managing occupancy, arming yourself with the financial data that indicate the impact of discounting is critical. If you are financially healthy and can create operational health for the team and children, then you might be able to provide greater than average discounts for staff and certain parent groups. Just be sure to make conscious decisions that are informational and fact-based to create the healthiest balance for your school.

I refer to discounting as our greatest hidden danger in managing the delicate balance of revenue and expenses. The reason it is a potential hidden danger is that most business owners are not armed with the information that helps them understand the impact of discounting. Many business owners only record the discounted tuition in their billing system. As a result, it is nearly impossible to quickly see the impact of your discounting decisions. The appropriate way to record income is to always record the current stated tuition rate and then record the discount in the billing system, giving you clear information about the financial impact of your discounting decisions. In times of greatly increasing salaries and operating costs, it is vital to know the impact of discounting decisions and what changes might be made quickly to steady the financial picture.

In addition, discounting tuition rates can sometimes lead to a perception in your community that your school offers lower-quality care compared to competitors that charge higher rates. This can be damaging to your school's reputation and may make it harder to attract families who value quality over price. While offering tuition discounts can be a tempting strategy for attracting and retaining families and a useful strategy in certain situations, it's essential to consider the potential pitfalls and long-term impacts on your school and to approach discounting with caution. Carefully consider the long-term impact on your school's finances, reputation, and ability to provide quality care before implementing any discounting strategies.

Common discounts include the following:

Staff Discounts

The majority of schools discount the cost of tuition for the children of their team members. The historic rule of thumb is free childcare for management team members and half-price childcare for teachers and other support staff. This strategy greatly improves the ability to attract and retain quality team members. There have been some initiatives to not discount infant and toddler programs, as these programs are likely at less than a breakeven point to begin with. Another strategy is to limit the number of children discounted per team member to two. But in this difficult hiring environment, I would use this discount liberally to support the team and to improve your ability to recruit. Another strategy is to align your team members with alternative subsidy tuition sources for their children if possible. This strategy alleviates the strain of the tuition and discount for both the school and the team member. At the present time, several states have invested in paying tuition for early education teachers, and many other states are considering this investment, minimizing the difficulty in hiring, financial stress on the teacher, and financial stress on the school. I personally *love* this investment!

Subsidy Discounts

As stated in Pillar Two, subsidy tuition (or tuition paid by a non-family source such as a government agency) is generally finite. A few states currently contribute the actual cost of care but most do not. Some states allow a contributing fee charged to parents to bridge the gap between the subsidy rate and the market rate, but owners often choose not to charge this fee because they perceive that families can't afford it or their competitors don't charge the difference, making competition challenging. This creates a difficult balance between revenue and the cost of care.

Vacation or "Free" Days

If your school is allowing enrolled students to take days off from school and not pay or pay discounted tuition, this is your first place to start in minimizing discounts. It is no longer industry norm to allow families to pay for only the days they choose to attend, as a business continues to have operating expenses, and a slot is being held, even if the child is absent for a day. The industry norm around this discount is to remove it completely. Even if your local competition gives vacation discounts, I suggest removing it. A good strategy is to implement a "smaller than necessary" tuition rate increase and eliminate a discount at the same time, as this coupling strategy could lead to a stronger financial picture than a larger tuition rate increase. As stated, be sure to communicate to families how and why you have chosen to change the tuition rate and eliminate discounts.

Discounts for Multiple Children in the Family

Historically, the majority of the industry has offered a discount for families that enroll more than one child, with a typical discount of 5-10% off of the tuition of the child(ren) with the lesser tuition rate. Recent trends have been to not offer this discount, though this trend is newer than eliminating vacation or free days. Consider the competition trend in your area, but don't hesitate to be the trendsetter!

Industry Discounts

Some business owners choose to discount the tuition for families that work for a particular business or in a particular industry. While I believe that the early education industry's long-term solution will include greater participation by businesses investing in their employees' childcare, my guiding question is: do you have a true partnership with the business? Is the business promoting your school to its employees? If the answer is no, then those families probably would have come to your school anyway. However, it is a great strategy to create a relationship with the business or industry you are discounting and let them know that you are providing a valuable benefit to their employees. Ask how they might contribute to the school to allow this to continue to happen. Can they pay the discounted portion on behalf of the employees? Can they promote the school to their team members? Can they cut your grass, send a maintenance technician periodically, contribute to supplies, etc.?

Military Discounts

Some business owners have a particular group of people that they choose to support with discounted tuition, such as military families. Again, there are no wrong decisions in personal choice; I just encourage business owners to make decisions armed with the information around the impact of the annual net revenue they are giving away that would have gone toward the collective health of the school.

Early Payment Discounts

Some schools choose to offer discounts to families paying a month or a year in advance, although much of the industry is moving toward monthly or annual tuition payments as standard in parent groups that can tolerate it. The common discount is 5-10%. I personally struggle with this discount because with our slim margins at 15-20%, which is needed to reinvest in the school—along with a lack of investment options available that would allow us to use the cash that is paid early to make more than 5-10%—it is difficult to justify the discount.

Enrollment Discounts

If families join your center primarily because of discounts, they may be more likely to leave once the discounts are no longer available, leading to fluctuations in enrollment and revenue. I don't have a clear preference on short-term discounts for enrollment (some schools promote a discounted month, or three months) as there are good examples of this strategy working well to promote an occupancy increase. At the same time, there are examples of difficulty in maintaining these enrollments once the discount runs out.

With her hard work on occupancy building and setting her tuition rates at a more healthy level, Harriet was taking some time off and cutting down on the amount of time she was in the school—with great success! The team began to thrive, feeling eager to learn and grow in their roles. With the new management position and more financial health, she was able to increase pay and found it easier to hire and support her teachers with more time off, as well as send them for advanced training. Her work-life balance felt more aligned, and she was sleeping better!

After learning about how to gain accurate information to make decisions around the impact of her policy setting, Harriet began to use her billing system as a valuable tool in managing her company. She began to record the full tuition in her billing system and then apply a discount, recording the discount by type, so she could see clearly the impact of her discounting decisions. Having accomplished these steps, she had the information that showed that she was discounting $80,000 annually in a combination of $60,000 for vacation days and $20,000 for staff discounts. Harriet knew that other local providers allowed families to not pay when their children didn't attend, but now that she was armed with the information about how much this was costing the school and how much she could do with the extra $60,000 a year, she decided to eliminate this discount and focus solely on discounts for her team's children. By eliminating vacation discounts, she decreased her total discounts from $80,000 to $20,000, adding $60,000 to the bottom line. The new net revenue was now $1,647,872.

Calculation

$1,587,872 former net revenue + $60,000 reduction in discounts = $1,647,872

What does this mean? Harriet now had $60,000 more in cash to improve salaries, possibly add health insurance or a new curriculum, or hire a Floater to relieve teachers and cover absences.

Discounting tuition rates can put a strain on your school's finances, especially if the discounts are not sustainable in the long run. If you offer discounts without carefully considering the impact on your bottom line, you may find yourself struggling to cover operating costs and maintain quality standards. Relying too heavily on tuition discounts to attract and retain families can lead to a volatile revenue stream.

In addition to creating cashflow and resource constraints, consistently offering discounts can dilute the perceived value of your early education center's brand. Families may come to see your school as a bargain option rather than a high-quality provider, affecting your ability to attract families willing to pay higher rates.

❧

Implementation Tips

Record your stated rate, less the discount by category, in your billing system. This will allow you to quickly see the financial impact of your decisions to discount tuition.

Over time, make it a goal to eliminate all discounts except staff.

Consider the elimination of one or more discounts in conjunction with a smaller tuition rate increase if you feel that your client base has limited ability to pay more tuition. Often eliminating a discount will get you closer to financial health than a larger tuition rate increase.

Consider grandfathering current families receiving discounts and eliminating the discount for new students if you are concerned about the impact on enrollment.

Help your staff receive subsidy support for their children's tuition when appropriate, improving their personal financial picture as well as the school's finances.

Educate stakeholders and decision-makers in your state about the value of contributing toward your staff's childcare.

Summary of Driving Revenue

The first three Pillars—occupancy, tuition rates, and discounts—all work together to create the revenue health of your school. It is important to consider all three when making decisions around enrollment, tuition rate setting, and increasing or decreasing discounts. The financial health of the school and its ability to serve families depend on it.

Chapter 7
Pillar Four—Salary Expense

Whew! This one's complicated! With Pillar Four, we are shifting to the expense side of our strategies. As we make that shift, remember that *no amount of cost control will ever get you to financial health* without a healthy amount of revenue. So, although the next strategies are important, they don't compare to having a healthy revenue that supports your necessary expenses. If you are not at 70% occupancy or above, charging a tuition rate that reflects the cost of care, and limiting discounts, stop reading here and focus on revenue-building strategies.

Since the beginning of my career in early education, I have said that *nothing* replaces creating an amazing work environment where people feel valued and respected and understand the value that they bring to children and that pay alone will not attract high quality teachers and support teams. That was true in 1986, and it is true today. This important challenge is not new; it has been the number one expense focus since my career began in the industry, and I'm sure it was also before my time! It has just increased during the most difficult period in the industry's history that we have ever experienced.

Before COVID-19, I said some ridiculous things to business owners about the best strategies to control staff costs, such as that their best strategies are to "combine age groups" or "send staff home when ratios allow and protect your core team." Phooey! Although those aren't terrible strategies and remain important, in today's environment and in building teams with the current work group, they are secondary to creating an amazing work experience, opportunities for advancement, opportunities to participate in meaningful work, and healthy pay.

A Focus on Culture Building

It might seem odd to start a chapter on staff cost management with a focus on culture building before cost control. But don't worry, we will get there. In the meantime, as stated, no amount of cost management strategizing will suffice if your team does not want to be there. There are several things I give COVID-19 credit for in terms of positively affecting our work environment, and one is that is that today's workforce demands meaningful work in environments that are challenging and supportive and where they have a sense of community with strong relationships, a supportive work-life balance, and opportunities for advancement. Again, we will never pay our way to financial health in this area. Pay alone will not attract and retain the team you want for your company. And who wants to be motivated solely by pay anyway? People are seeking meaningful, purposeful work, strong connections, and appreciation. And guess what? Those things can be low cost or free to create, as well as being so much fun! So, although this chapter is focused on managing the ability to control the financial picture, it is necessary to couple that with creating a culture that high-quality teams want to work and thrive in.

Consider the following opportunities for creating positive culture:

1. **Positive Work Environment**
   a. Foster a supportive and collaborative culture.
   b. Encourage collaboration and open communication among staff members.
   c. Recognize and celebrate achievements and milestones.

2. **Support Systems**
   a. Provide resources for managing stress and maintaining work/life balance.
   b. Offer counselling and support services when needed.
   c. Create a culture where teachers feel comfortable seeking help and support.

3. **Open Communication and Feedback**
   a. Establish regular check-ins and feedback sessions.
   b. Encourage teachers to share their ideas and concerns.
   c. Implement suggestions and show appreciation for their input.

    d. Implement performance reviews to identify areas of improvement and reward high-performing staff.

4. **Flexible Scheduling**
   a. Offer flexible work schedules to accommodate staffs' personal needs.
   b. Provide options for part-time or job-sharing arrangements.

5. **Work/Life Balance Programs**
   a. Implement wellness programs to promote physical and mental well-being.
   b. Encourage teachers to take advantage of their paid time off and have sufficient support staff to cover their job duties.
   c. Organize team-building activities and social events to foster a sense of community.

6. **Professional Development Opportunities**
   a. Offer ongoing training and development programs.
   b. Support teachers in pursuing further education and certifications.
   c. Provide access to workshops, conferences, and networking opportunities.

7. **Career Advancement and Recognition**
   a. Provide clear pathways for career advancement within your school and promote from within.
   b. Recognize and reward teachers for their hard work and achievements.
   c. Celebrate accomplishments and milestones publicly.

A Focus on Cost Control

As we know, the largest expense for an early education business is staff payroll. In a normalized period when we are able to charge the cost of care, salaries alone, excluding other staff costs, will comprise on average 42-48% of all tuition dollars paid. This includes salaries for the team only with their regular pay, holiday and PTO pay, and overtime pay—not including the owner, unless the owner is also the director. Once you include payroll taxes, benefits, training, and recruiting costs, total costs serving teams are on average 50-55% of all tuition dollars paid. This heavy expense load makes it critical to balance necessary hours of instruction and care with revenue sources to support them.

It is important to think about this expense load as a percentage of net revenue (a variable and not fixed expense), and not as a fixed number, because as enrollment and revenue change, it is necessary to quickly adjust hours and related costs up or down to match. A fixed number ignores changes in enrollment that might mean you are under- or over-staffing when a change occurs.

Recent shifts in employee expectations have changed how we are now thinking about staff costs. A June 2024 HINGE survey of providers revealed the following:

How much have your pay rates have risen since COVID-19? The results were as follows:

21-30% of providers stated	40% increase in wages
31-50%	28%
1-20%	22%
Over 50%	8%
None	2%

What is your primary strategy for controlling staff costs? The results were as follows:

Monitoring Hours	46%
Allowing Staff to Go Home Early	25%
Monitoring Pay Rates	19%
Other	10%

Further, when asked the method for controlling staff costs, the results were as follows:

Manually	39.9%
As a Percent of Revenue	36.4%
As a Dollar Amount	11.6%
With a Computer Program	5.8%
Other	6.4%

When asked what other strategies were useful in controlling staff costs, of those responding:

Using Floaters	67%
Using Assistant Team Members	63%
More Support for Directors	30%
Limiting Management Teams in the Classroom	27%

Other strategies mentioned included raising tuition rates, combining classes at the end of the day, using administrative teams as subs, and outsourcing to virtual assistants.

I am not personally a fan of regularly using directors and administrative teams in the classroom. However, these are not normalized environments and emergencies happen. Design your staff schedule to cover classrooms with trained and talented teachers, plan for your usual need for substitutes to cover vacations and absences, and preserve the management team for supporting teachers, parents and children; hiring and training; and enrolling. Stressing management teams will lead to issues in the school and a lesser focus on necessary enrollment that drives the revenue to support them.

A percentage of revenue is all that matters! Staff payroll and related costs follow the number of children you are providing care for, so budgeting and tracking based on a percentage of revenue is the only logical method for cost management. Tracking as a dollar amount ignores the possibility of fast occupancy changes that occur during transitional periods such as school year to summer and during times of increased competition that might lead to occupancy drops, or even decreased competition that leads to occupancy increases. Historically, I have used a benchmark of spending 45% of net revenue (tuition income plus other charges less discounts) on staff pay at 70% occupancy. Lower staff cost percentages can be gained at higher occupancies, and it is nearly impossible to maintain this budget at lower occupancies. This benchmark includes a director and assistant director— either part-time or full-time depending on the size of the school—and all teaching and support staff, including regular pay, overtime, holiday, and vacation pay. It does not include owner pay, unless that owner is also the director. Although I hesitate to encourage any business owner to overspend to the point of stressing the financial balance of the school, I also must admit that we have never seen a time that is more difficult in terms of balancing the cost of staff with what parents can pay.

In this time of unprecedented increases in staff pay, I am asked regularly if I will adjust my benchmark for the staff salaries cost structure. The short answer is—no. In the short run we can stress our financial model, but in the long run that is not sustainable. If the model breaks down, businesses fail, and then there is no care for anyone. Since we have reportedly experienced at least 30% increases in wages, with some reporting as much as 50% since the beginning of the COVID-19 pandemic, balancing the new cost of care with tuition rates is even more critical than ever. Realizing that there is a limit to what parents can afford to pay, some more than others, until we get outside help, the model will continue to be difficult.

I am often asked, "How much can I pay my staff?" My short answer is "As much as possible!" What I mean is that we all want our teachers and support staff to make a great wage, not be financially stressed, and be able to support themselves and their families. Our mission as business owners is to balance the competitive wage with hours (or days) spent and revenue derived from tuition rates. Often when I encounter an owner struggling to balance salaries as a healthy percentage of income, the answer is not that they are overspending on pay rates or hours, but that the tuition rates are not sufficient to cover the cost of care.

In addition to salaries, employer portions of payroll taxes also add to the expense load. The employer is responsible for half of the employee social security and Medicare, and all the employees' federal and state unemployment. Because these three expenses add another 9.5 to 10% to the payroll, overspending on payroll means overspending on payroll taxes as well. Other staff costs include benefits such as health insurance and retirement plans, training and certifications, recruiting costs and background checks, and the necessary costs of creating fun and engaging work experiences.

Consider the following opportunities for cost control:

1. **Manage Hours**
   a. Implement a planning tool that assists in setting schedules for your staff to align with children's schedules and required ratios.
   b. Combine age groups in the early morning and late afternoon when appropriate and healthy for the children.
   c. Execute "management by walking around" to manage times when ratios allow for staff to leave early or to combine classes.
   d. Eliminate overtime! A healthy substitute teaching team might cost more per hour, but less if it eliminates overtime.
   e. Engage the team in notifying management when ratios align with one team member leaving early. Today's workforce values their personal time!

2. **Offer Competitive Compensation and Benefits**
   a. Conduct market research to offer competitive salaries.
   b. Provide comprehensive benefits packages including paid time off, free or reduced child care for the children of team members, and health insurance.
   c. Consider additional perks such as tuition reimbursement for additional degrees and wellness programs.

3. **Utilize Substitutes, Volunteers, and Interns**
   a. Use part-time or substitute teachers to manage peak periods or unexpected absences.
   b. Partner with local colleges and universities for internships.
   c. Create volunteer programs for community members as support in the classroom, if licensing allows, or for administrative support.
   d. Use volunteers and interns to support teachers and reduce workload outside of classroom ratio.

4. **Create a Detailed Budget**
   a. Develop a comprehensive budget that includes all salary-related expenses as a percentage of Net Revenue.
   b. Monitor actual expenses against the budget regularly.
   c. Adjust the budget as needed to reflect changes in enrollment or staffing.

5. **Plan for Seasonal Variations**
   a. Anticipate and plan for seasonal fluctuations in enrollment.
   b. Adjust staffing levels and expenses to match enrollment patterns.
   c. Use seasonal budgeting to ensure financial stability throughout the year.

6. **Leverage Technology for Efficiency**
   a. Use software solutions for scheduling, payroll, and administrative tasks.
   b. Automate billing and communication to reduce the need for additional administrative staff.
   c. Invest in training staff to efficiently use technological tools.

7. **Cross-Train Staff**
   a. Train teachers and support staff to perform multiple roles.
   b. Encourage flexibility and adaptability within the team.
   c. Use cross-training to cover absences without the need for additional hires.
   d. Exposure to other positions can provide opportunities for career advancement, increasing job satisfaction and reducing turnover.

8. **Implement Performance-Based Compensation**
   a. Introduce performance-based bonuses or incentives.
   b. Tie compensation to measurable outcomes, such performance metrics and enrollment.
   c. Ensure that performance metrics are clear, achievable, and transparent.
9. **Evaluate Outsourcing Options**
   a. Consider a specialized staffing source for hiring and for substitute teachers.
   b. Consider outsourcing cleaning to eliminate this chore from the teachers' day.
10. **Know the Cost of Turnover**
    a. Calculate your cost of turnover.
    b. Understand the impact on children and families when staff leave.
    c. Compare the cost of turnover with the cost of increased pay.

A Focus on Staffing Processes

The hiring, onboarding, and retention processes associated with gaining and maintaining teams are important in creating compelling work opportunities, making staff feel secure, and reducing turnover.

Consider the following basic staffing processes:

1. **Managing Hiring Processes**
   a. Define your ideal candidate with the qualities, skills, and experience you are looking or in a candidate. Consider education, experience working with children, personality traits, and culture fit with your team,
   b. Craft compelling job descriptions outlining the roles and responsibilities required.
   c. Highlight the unique benefits and opportunities your center offers emphasizing the impact teachers will have on children's lives.
   d. Emphasize the FUN they will have in the school and that there is no night and weekend work!
2. **Utilizing Multiple Recruitment Channels**
   a. Post job openings on popular job boards and early education websites.
   b. Leverage social media platforms to reach a wider audience.
   c. Network with local colleges, universities, and teacher training programs.
3. **Streamlining the Hiring Process**
   a. Simplify the application process to encourage more candidates to apply.

    b. Implement a thorough yet efficient interview process.

    c. Provide timely feedback and communicate regularly with candidates.

4. **Screening Candidates Carefully**

    a. Review resumes and cover letters and conduct initial phone interviews to ensure that possible team members meet your basic requirements.

    b. Contact previous employers and supervisors to get a sense of the candidates' performance and reliability.

    c. Conduct in-depth interviews with candidates to assess their qualifications, skills, and fit with your center's culture, and ask behavorial questions to gauge how they would or have managed situations common in early education settings.

5. **Onboarding and Mentorship**

    a. Develop a comprehensive onboarding program to help new teachers integrate smoothly.

    b. Provide adequate training before launching the new hire into a classroom on their own!

    c. Pair new teachers with experience mentors for guidance and support.

    d. Create a welcoming and inclusive atmosphere from day one.

Harriet's original dream was to hire the best teachers, and she knew that she would need to pay them more than her competition to attract the best. She also understood that hiring decisions would be important, but early on she didn't understand how hard it would be to balance her staff costs with quality programming and financial health. Before she knew to focus on occupancy to build a stronger revenue stream and eliminate discounts that were no longer industry norm, she had a terrible time controlling costs at a healthy percentage of revenue, constantly wondered how else she could cut costs, and lacked the team she needed to adequately manage the school and focus on enrollment. Harriet was spending $695,000 annually for her team's salaries, which included overtime, holiday pay, and PTO pay. Her salary position looked like this:

Calculation

$695,000 / $1,200,000 former net revenue = .5792 or 57.92%

What does this mean? Of all the net revenue Harriet was earning in her school, she was spending 57.92% of that on staff salaries.

Harriet learned that she would always struggle to have the team she needed to adequately create the high quality and stable environment she was dreaming of if she didn't figure out how to get this important metric in line. Initially thinking that she was doing something wrong with cost control, she felt that she was just running in circles analyzing pay rates, managing hours, sending staff home early, covering them in the classroom herself, and still not having the time to focus on high-quality programming and enrolling.

Once Harriet made revenue-building her focus rather than trying to cost-control her way out of the problem, she took a risk on hiring a director for an annual salary of $80,000 and re-directed herself to running the business, strategizing enrollment, and supporting the team and families better. With the net revenue increase generated by a higher occupancy, increasing tuition rates to a cost of care rate, and eliminating some unnecessary discounts, she actually increased the salaries but was now in a more stable position.

New Calculation
$$\$775,000 \,/\, \$1,647,872 = .47 \text{ or } 47\%$$

Harriet increased her spending on salaries by $80,000 with the new director position and saw that although she was spending more, she was also earning more. She had reduced the salary percent to 47% of net income. She knew that this was slightly higher than the targeted benchmark of 45%, and she would continue to work on strengthening her net income within the tolerance level of her customers' ability and desire to pay the cost of care tuition rate.

Harriet was on a roll! She implemented staff cost management systems that included planning staff schedules to align with children's schedules, and she trained her management and teaching teams to continually monitor ratios so that someone might take advantage of the ability to go home early, saving the school resources and improving the work/life balance for those team members interested in more personal time. A win-win for all!

Knowing the strategies that work in your school and program is the foundation of community building and cost management. Everyone wants managers, teachers, and support staff to be paid well, have excellent benefits, have fun work environments with advancement opportunities, and love coming to work. We also want parents not to be financially stressed and for children to receive the high-quality care and education that they deserve.

The balance between all of these goals is important in managing a financially stable school. Develop and maintain basic staffing strategies and experiment with alternative strategies that focus spending on what matters most in your core teaching hours. Maintain the intention of the management team on supporting teachers and families, training and developing the team, and driving revenue and necessary administrative tasks. Experiment with alternative strategies that might be impactful in managing costs. And do not underestimate the value of the fifteen minutes of payroll savings that also means a valuable team member gets to go home early!

❧

Implementation Tips

Are you correcting the right problem? If you are struggling to get your staff costs as a percentage of revenue in line, is cost control the main issue? Or is the revenue you are comparing the costs with sufficient for the actual cost of care? No amount of cost control will get you healthy if the revenue is not sufficient to align with what it costs to operate your business.

When cost control is an issue, the problem is rarely that you are overpaying in terms of wages. Usually, the problem is in hours spent that you could tweak here or there. Although it is important to preserve the team's hours and ability to support themselves and their families, they also might appreciate leaving early when ratios allow. Don't underestimate the power of the fifteen-minute savings when possible and healthy for the class.

Consider allowing management staff to work from home one day a week on administrative tasks to lessen the stress of their work and create a greater work/life balance. Be sure that the school is appropriately managed on-site during their absence.

Develop a system of "management by walking around" and train the team to notify management when ratios allow for a team member to go home early.

Make the workplace a fun and engaging place to be. A caring environment starts with you and contagiously spreads through the school!

Chapter 8

Pillar Five—Rent or Mortgage Costs

Your facility is not just a building—it is an investment opportunity! The fifth and final Pillar is the second largest expense for the average early education center: the rent or mortgage payments. Unless you are delivering a virtual program, there must be a facility that houses your care and education. Businesses, and the real estate they are located in, are two completely different assets that are each treated differently, strategized differently, and potentially bought and sold differently.

One option, owning the facility that you operate in, allows you control over your facility and your expenses. I'm a big fan of the opportunity that owning real estate brings. Over time, real estate is generally an asset that appreciates, a good source of cashflow, and a solid tax strategy. However, owning real estate is resource-intensive, and to the extent that you don't have those resources, they may put a strain on the business's financial picture or prevent the growth that you and your team might be seeking. In this case, leasing might be a better option.

Leasing is a great option when you are getting started or in times of fast growth, both typical times with limited resources. Using the landlord's money to invest in the real estate, improve the facility, or grow into new buildings is a great strategy for preserving cash and growing.

How Much Rent Can I Pay?

Rent costs are critical to align with healthy benchmarks when purchasing a facility or negotiating a lease at a market rate that is not just indicative of the local market but also balanced with the potential revenue of the school. This is often a confusing concept for landlords and tenants who rely solely on market appraisals and comps for other real estate in their area in setting rents or real estate value. When there is a business operating in a building, the ability of the business to generate the revenue sufficient to pay a certain amount in rent is all that matters. Sometimes the building's ability to gain rent and the potential sales value outpaces the business's ability to pay rent, such as in times of sharply increasing value in the area's real estate. When this happens, the landlord might make the decision to accept lesser rent than market value to allow the school to balance its financial metrics. Alternatively, the business owner may make the decision to move to another facility that is more in line with what the business can afford. At other times, the school's real estate value can be in an area that is decreasing in value for reasons that might include being in an area that is not growing. In this case, coupled with continued demand for early education in the area and the desire to stay in the same building, the rent can be adjusted down.

For our benchmarking, rent does not include repairs, insurance, or property taxes, commonly referred to as a triple net (NNN) lease. Ratios for rent to net income can vary but hover around the range of 12-15% when the school is 70% occupied. There are some outliers that also work. Some programs are housed in older facilities and the rent can be as low at 6-10% of revenue. These programs usually will then spend more on maintenance and shift the lower rent savings into lower tuition rates for families or for parent groups funded primarily by subsidy systems that can be finite and lower than market cost of care. Another outlier is programs that run consistently over 80-90% occupancy and choose to spend more rent for a much higher quality facility. Both scenarios work, but should be done consciously, making decisions around what to spend and what the impact is on the school's overall financial health. The key is to calculate the market rent at 70% occupancy and use that to gauge the building's ability to pay rent.

Another circumstance that some business owners are able to take advantage of is a donated or below-market rate facility, such as a church, public school, or other facility that is provided for below market rent or for free. Those operators usually choose to shift the budget allocated for rent payments to providing lower tuition rates for families, higher pay rates for staff, or a combination of both. This situation is excellent in shifting the cost load to higher quality, but it is not the reality for the majority of business owners.

Do the Metrics Matter if I Pay Myself Rent?

Most business owners who also own the real estate that their business operates in hold the real estate and business in separate entities, paying themselves rent. We often get the question from business owners about how much rent they can pay themselves. The answer is based on what is best for them from a tax perspective, and that answer is much better coming from a tax professional. From a company and real estate value perspective, the answer is that it doesn't matter. When selling a business or real estate, the Transaction Advisor will set the rent at a market level, so what rent you have historically paid yourself does not matter in setting business and real estate value for a future sale.

What Other Facility Costs Should I Consider?

Other cost considerations for managing your school are repairs, maintenance, janitorial, insurance, property taxes, telephone, internet, and pest control, with the full load of facility costs for most schools ranging around 22-25% of net revenue.

What Should I Think About for Maintaining the Facility?

The quality, maintenance, branding, and aesthetically pleasing look of the facility's exterior and interior should not be discounted as one of the most important marketing tools for building enrollment. It is regularly cited as the first draw for prospective customers into the school. It is necessary to maintain the facility with safe and inviting environments, with maintenance and repairs being only the baseline of healthy standards. Remodelling should be an investment that is planned for and implemented at least every ten years to generate interest in the school and compete with "new and shiny" facilities that enter the market and offer initial appeal to parents. I love the strategy to execute a complete remodel all at once to gain a "wow" factor, as opposed to one small remodel at a time for items such as flooring, painting, and signage, but budgetary constraints might prevent this option (see more on partnerships with landlords or lenders). Although small projects can be impressive, they lack the impact that a complete remodel attracts.

Should I Lease or Own?

Deciding whether to lease or own a building for your childcare center is a significant decision that impacts your financial planning, operational flexibility, and long-term growth. Both options have their advantages and disadvantages, and the best choice depends on your specific circumstances and business goals. One of the most confusing decisions for any business owner is whether to lease or buy the facility from which you operate. The answer to this question typically evolves as the company grows and builds capital—and as the owner makes moves to preserve that capital—but there is no one correct answer. Everyone must consider their own capital needs and business strategy, but there are clear pros and cons to both options. Here are some considerations I suggest you think about.

I love real estate ownership, but real estate ownership takes resources, and resources are needed for growth. In my experience, to keep a top-level team engaged and excited, you have to continue to create opportunities for them, which necessitates growth. So, the trade-off is if you want to own your real estate, it's a great way to build wealth and save taxes, but it takes resources. If you want to lease, you can preserve those resources for growth. But now you have a partner in your business because someone else is in control of the real estate.

Many operators do a combination of these, and real estate can be used effectively in growing a company. Strategies include selling your existing real estate and using the funds to purchase a new or existing facility to grow in to. It's easier to sell a mature, cash-flowing property than sell or get a loan for a new, unestablished building. Another benefit of this growth strategy is that it can be done in a tax-deferred manner. Another option is to sell the business and keep the real estate as a revenue stream, with a solid operator/tenant in the building. Whatever your future goals, begin to think about your real estate as a separate asset from your business. They both should contribute to your personal financial health.

Leasing Your Real Estate

As both a landlord (I currently own or invest in twelve early education facilities that are leased to operators) and a tenant (currently on the HINGE office space), I can say confidently that both landlords and tenants want the same thing: a long, stable relationship. Landlords are looking for tenants who are doing great work and have a long, stable business that generates a healthy rent stream. Tenants are looking for landlords that are fair, supportive of their businesses, and possibly able to help the tenants grow.

I have experienced some great landlord/tenant collaborations personally, and here are a couple of examples. In the first few weeks of navigating COVID-19 threats, I got an important call from one of my tenants. "We are not going to pay you rent for the next six months," they said. *Good for you!* I thought. *I want you to still be here as my tenant when this craziness is over.* I immediately called my mortgage lender and said, "Hey! My tenant is not paying me rent for the next six months. What can I do?" The answer I received was: "Don't pay your mortgage payments for that time period."

Another important communication came earlier in the relationship with my tenant when I got this call: "We would like to update the facility to stay ahead of local competition who is building brand new schools in our area. Can you give us $250,000 to do that? We will increase the rent in exchange." *Great!* I thought. *I want my facility to be well-maintained and up-to-date.* I went to my mortgage lender and said that I would like to borrow an additional $250,000 against my mortgage. Since my loan-to-value ratio was now lower than the bank threshold, it was an easy ask. I received the money and passed it along to my tenant; they updated the building, and more enrollment was attracted, increasing the viability of the business and the security of my tenant. I am now looking for more opportunities to partner with my tenant on additional properties. Everyone wants the same thing! Landlord/tenant relationships are important to the long-term health and for growth opportunities for your business.

The following are the benefits of leasing:

1. **Lower Initial Costs.** Leasing typically requires less upfront capital than purchasing a property. Initial costs usually include a security deposit and the first month's rent, which can be more manageable for new businesses or those with limited capital.

2. **Predictable Expenses.** Leases often provide more predictable monthly expenses, making budgeting easier. Rent payments are usually fixed or increase at an expected rate for the lease term, which helps in financial planning.

3. **Flexibility to Relocate.** Leasing provides the flexibility to relocate more easily if your business needs change. At the end of the lease term, you can move to a different location that better suits your requirements. An example would be operating in a geographic area where the customer base is aging and no longer supporting an early education population.

4. **Easier Expansion.** Leasing can make it easier to expand your business. If you need more space, you might negotiate additional lease terms or relocate to a larger property without the complications or risk of selling a building.

5. **Maintenance Responsibility.** Depending on the terms of the lease, the landlord might be responsible for at least the structure and possibly major systems of the building, reducing your operational burdens. In some situations, the landlord could also be responsible for other maintenance costs, and this is usually reflected in a higher lease rate.

6. **Less Financial Risk.** Leasing minimizes financial risk, as you are not tied to a long-term mortgage. If your business faces unexpected challenges, you have the flexibility to downsize or relocate more easily.

7. **Market Fluctuations.** Leasing protects you from market fluctuations in property values. You are not exposed to the risk of your property decreasing in value, which can impact your financial stability.

8. **Relationship Building for Potential Growth.** A strong relationship with your landlord is an excellent way to grow. Ask the landlord for new opportunities or present them with new opportunities to expand the relationship. Use your landlord's capital for facility upgrades.

Owning Your Real Estate

Owning your real estate can be a great investment opportunity over time. While operating the school that is housed in your building, you are growing wealth in the value of the real estate as well as receiving potential tax benefits and enjoying control over the property. Options to use your real estate by selling it and maintaining the business can bring valuable resources for growth. Conversely, selling the business and maintaining the real estate with a stable tenant operating the business can alleviate the stress of operating the business and allow for long-term passive cashflow.

The advantages of owning your real estate include the following:

1. **Control Over the Property.** Owning the building gives you complete control over modifications, renovations, and the overall use of the space. This can be particularly important for customizing the facility to meet specific regulatory requirements and educational standards. This can include building additional classrooms, creating specialized play areas, or adding other amenities that enhance your childcare center's appeal.

2. **Building Equity.** Owning a property allows you to build equity over time. Mortgage payments contribute to asset ownership, which can be financially beneficial.

3. **Potential Tax Benefits.** Property ownership can offer tax advantages, such as deductions for mortgage interest and depreciation.

4. **Asset Appreciation.** While ownership comes with market risk, it also offers the potential for property value appreciation. This can provide significant financial benefits if the real estate market performs well.

5. **Long-Term Investment.** Owning your property is a long-term investment that can diversify your financial portfolio and provide security for you and your business. If you are open to the idea of retaining ownership of your real estate when you exit your business, you can create a cashflow stream for your future.

The decision to lease or own your childcare building hinges on a variety of factors, including financial resources, long-term business goals, and operational needs. While I am personally a big fan of owning real estate, resource constraints and your long-term company goals will dictate where your cash is best spent. If you have a growth mentality, and resources are limited, then using them for real estate ownership might not be the best strategy. If you want to build your investment in the current facility you have, then owning or trying to purchase the facility you have with your excess cash might be a good investment that could give you ownership options beyond owning and operating the business. Leasing offers lower initial costs, flexibility, and possible reduced maintenance responsibilities, making it an attractive option for new or rapidly growing businesses. On the other hand, owning a property provides control, stability, and the potential for long-term financial gains, making it suitable for established businesses with a strong financial foundation.

Harriet had worked hard to align her school's revenue stream with healthy benchmarks and felt proud of all that she had accomplished! With processes for continual evaluation of occupancy and enrollment opportunities, along with daily staff cost management and semi-annual evaluation of her tuition rates and discounts, Harriet wondered if her rent cost was working well for her. Her initial strategy was to be in an area that was growing with a customer base that seemed eager to invest in early education for their children, and in a facility that maximized space and was visible and attractive to drive-by traffic. When she started, she compared the rent to other retail spaces in the area and learned from a local broker that it was in line with the market. Now that she understood early education benchmarks, she wondered if her leased facility was working for the financial health of her business or against it. She reviewed the benchmarks and calculated the following.

Her business generated the following annual revenue at the benchmark of 70% occupancy:

110 licensed capacity * $347 average weekly tuition rate * 52 weeks * .7 or 70% occupancy = $1,389,388 annual net revenue

Her rent was $265,000 annually.

Calculation
$265,000 annual rent / $1,389,388 annual net revenue at 70% occupancy = .1907 or 19%

Harriet learned that true "market" rent was driven by her business's ability to pay rent and not necessarily what other industries were paying for similar buildings in her area. She also understood that paying rent at 15% of 70% occupancy was a healthy benchmark. With her rent at 19% of net revenue when she was 70% full, she calculated that her rent would have created a more stable financial picture for the school if it had been in the $210,000 range.

Calculation

$1,389,388 annual net revenue at 70% * .15 or

15% rent = $208,408 in annual rent

Harriet planned to ask her landlord if she would either lower the rent in exchange for a longer term lease, invest in an expansion of the school, or help Harriet seek a second facility to expand into, since Harriet had several eager team members trained and ready for advancement opportunities. She realized that she had grown the team well and that she was in danger of losing them unless she could continue to give them opportunities to grow. And her new director would love to eventually grow to be an Area Manager over several schools—how exciting!

Rent is one of the most significant fixed costs for any business, including early education centers. Setting the right rent costs can be a balancing act that influences profitability, operational efficiency, and the quality of services provided. Starting a company with an imbalance in the rent percentage to revenue is a difficult situation to recover from. Once the facility is constructed or leased, it is difficult the change the mortgage or rent structure.

Implementation Tips

Use the Framework App to test your rent against your current ability to earn revenue at 70% occupancy and understand whether you are in a healthy range or not. Be sure your rent on a NNN basis is at or less than 15% of the revenue you can earn at 70% occupancy, unless you can consistently operate at high occupancies and you are willing to take the risk of a decline in enrollment.

Use the landlord's money! When it's time for a remodel, ask your landlord to invest the necessary funds in exchange for increased rent.

Use your landlord relationship for growth! Once you are established as a stable, reliable tenant, ask your landlord for new opportunities to lease from them or present opportunities yourself that they can invest in.

Re-negotiate your mortgage when appropriate. Just like landlords, lenders want a stable tenant who is secure in making the mortgage payments.

Maintain the facility in top condition. Be sure the exterior is pleasing and makes the right statement to those driving by.

Consider a complete remodel every ten years and if you are able, fund and implement the remodel all at once to create the "wow" factor and stay current with new competition.

Summary of Expense Management Pillars

The fourth and fifth Pillars, Salary Cost and Rent or Mortgage Costs, comprise the majority of all dollars spent to create a strong program in the average early education business. Of all revenue earned, these two expenses make up at least 55-60% of all tuition dollars paid in the average school. Focusing on strategies to align Salary Cost and Rent or Mortgage Cost before focusing on the many line items is a solid business practice. Getting these two expenses in healthy alignment with revenue is critical to success.

Part III

Building a
Sustainable Future

Chapter 9
Other Revenue Sources

While the first three Pillars—occupancy, tuition rates, and discounts—create the majority of the revenue stream in an early education business, there are other traditional charges that help supplement the revenue and contribute toward a stronger financial health.

Consider the following possible additional revenue sources:

Registration Fees

An annual registration fee is a charge that parents pay when they first enroll their child in a childcare program, and once a year thereafter. This fee is separate from the regular tuition and is typically used to cover administrative costs, supplies, and enhanced program quality. It can also serve as a commitment fee, ensuring that families are serious about enrolling their child for the upcoming year. With thoughtful planning and clear communication, annual registration fees can be a valuable tool in sustaining and improving a childcare business.

Considerations in setting registration fees include:

1. **Fee Amount.** Determining the appropriate fee amount is important. It should be high enough to cover necessary expenses but not so high that it becomes a burden for families. As with tuition rates, don't hesitate to be the trend setter in your market.

2. **Transparency.** Clear communication about the purpose and use of the registration fee is essential. Parents should understand what the fee covers and how it benefits their child's experience at the school.
3. **Timing.** Decide when the registration fee will be charged. Many centers collect it at the time of enrollment and re-enrollment each year.
4. **Refund Policy.** Establish a refund policy for the registration fee. While it's common for these fees to be non-refundable, being upfront about this policy can prevent misunderstandings and disputes.
5. **Combine with Other Fees.** Some centers combine the registration fee with other annual fees such as supply fees or activity fees. This can simplify the payment process for families and reduce the number of separate charges they need to manage.

If you are not charging a registration fee annually, this is a good place to start utilizing supplemental fees to support your school's financial health.

USDA Food Program

The United States Department of Agriculture (USDA) Food Program, officially known as the Child and Adult Care Food Program (CACFP), is a federal initiative that plays a crucial role in promoting nutritious meals and snacks for children and adults in care settings for schools that qualify. For childcare centers, participating in the CACFP not only helps ensure that children receive balanced, healthy meals but also provides financial assistance to support these efforts.

Schools qualify based on the family income of the population served in the school. In most qualified schools, the reimbursements will cover the cost of food, which is typically 5-6% of annual net revenue. Although the administrative burden to implement the program can be daunting, if you do not have the team resources to accurately report and invoice for reimbursement, consider outsourcing this task to a specialized provider who can do it for you.

Late Payment Fees

Managing finances in an early education program can be challenging, especially when it comes to ensuring timely tuition payments from parents. An effective strategy to encourage prompt payments and maintain cash flow is to implement and consistently enforce a late payment policy.

The primary purpose of late payment fees is to motivate parents to pay tuition on time, which helps ensure consistent cash flow for the school, contributing to the financial stability and enabling better planning and budgeting. Equally importantly, by reducing the number of late payments, administrative staff can spend less time on follow-ups and more time on other essential tasks such as teacher and program support.

Be sure that the fee is significant enough to encourage timely payments, that you clearly communicate the late payment fee policy to parents during the enrollment process and in written agreements, and that you apply the late payment policy consistently for all families. At the same time, be prepared to offer flexibility in cases of genuine financial hardship, prioritizing families who are communicating and following up and not sending Grandma in for pick-up to avoid talking to you.

When possible, consider using automated billing systems that send reminders and notifications to parents, and move toward monthly billing and automatic draft payments, if possible, in your parent group.

Late Pickup Fees

Implement a policy of charging a fee after the stated school closing time for late pickups. The cost associated with a late pickup—including possible staff overtime, infringing on staff personal time, and a possible upsetting experience for the child—makes charging a meaningful late fee a good idea. A typical fee is a dollar a minute after closing time. As with late payment fees, charge consistently and also be prepared with flexibility for situations that are unexpected with valued long-term customers.

Grants

Grant funds have been abundant since the COVID-19 pandemic, with most of the federal sources ending as support has shifted to state initiatives. In addition to government support, grants are available from businesses and non-profit organizations. Engage an interested team member or outsource to a professional grant seeker/writer to research and apply for grant funding. It is important to know what is available in your community, from the employers that families work for, and from the state you operate in, and to be timely in accessing opportunities for grants that might support expenses such as staff costs, facility improvement, or growth.

Fundraisers

Fundraisers are an excellent way to generate additional revenue, engage the community, and enhance the resources and programs offered to children. The most successful fundraisers tend to be for a specific stated purpose such as new playground equipment, educational materials, or facility improvements. When planning a fundraiser, ask for a team volunteer to lead the initiative, getting the collective team's ideas and buy-in. The event should have clear goals and a specific purpose. It is important to promote the event, track progress, acknowledge contributions, and celebrate success!

Facility Rent

One effective way to maximize the use of your facility is by renting your building for other purposes during off-hours. Many early education buildings can be used during evenings or weekends to supplement income and provide additional community outreach. Some common rental opportunities include churches, birthday parties, fitness or professional meetings. Some considerations when deciding to rent your facility are insurance and liability, security, compliance with existing leases or local regulations, and wear and tear on the building, as well as possibly the team. Hosting different groups and events can introduce your location to potential new families, increasing enrollment opportunities.

છ

Implementation Tips

Adding or increasing annual registration fees in conjunction with a smaller tuition rate increase can be a good strategy for increasing revenue.

Investigate the USDA Food Program for your school and, if you qualify, either add the administrative resources to your team or outsource to a company specializing in program administration.

Be sure that your policies for late payments and late pickups are sufficient to largely prevent them from happening. Charge the fees consistently, and be prepared for occasional flexibility when appropriate.

Have someone on the team specialize in grant funding by staying in close contact with grant sources, researching and writing, and tracking the success of grants. Government sources, businesses, and charitable organizations are all sources to consider.

Consider fundraising for a specific purpose. Ask the team and families what they are interested in supporting and communicate the success by showing the results!

Chapter 10
Other Expense Strategies

Most expense control issues that have the potential to stabilize or destabilize a school can be found Salaries or Rent and Mortgage Costs. I can literally count on one hand (um, one finger) the number of times that I thought a business owner might get in big trouble from expense control that didn't relate to either Staff Cost management or alignment with Rent or Mortgage Cost.

At the same time, slight shifts in other categories can bring additional resources to the school. The following strategies relating to other expense items could contribute valuable resources to make the overall financial picture easier to manage.

Food Costs

For most schools that provide two snacks and lunch, the related expense ranges at 5-6% of Net Revenue. Some schools have shifted to having parents provide lunch, citing closer alignment with children's preferences and cultures. This strategy eliminates the need for more expensive team members such as chefs and cooks and allows this reduction in spending to apply to other expenses such as increased teacher pay rates. Alternatively, some schools promote organic or healthy meals as a market differentiator, driving tuition rates to a higher level. Of course, not providing full meals is not an option for schools participating in the USDA food program.

Marketing Costs

Over time, marketing costs have decreased with more investment in less expensive options like digital and online options that reach possible customers. These options often require outsourcing since the skills to develop and implement these strategies are specialized.

Automated Billing, Payment, and Communication Systems

The sophistication of systems to support billing, tuition collection, and parent communication has increased rapidly since COVID-19, allowing a school to streamline administrative processes. This frees up staff, who are then able to focus on more important functions within the school. Also, today's parent group seeks easier payment methods and values frequent feedback on their children's days.

Supplies and Services

Purchases for food, paper goods, classrooms supplies and materials, along with services like cleaning, lawn care, and maintenance, should be price compared at least annually to ensure the quality and cost remain competitive. This is a great task to delegate to an eager team member.

Field Trips and Activity Fees

Fees for field trips and outside activities (and sometimes inside activities) should cover the cost of the event for the student as well as transportation and other related costs. Fees can be charged per event, monthly, or annually.

Insurance

Insurance coverage has become increasingly volatile in the last few years, with many experiencing the loss of certain coverages or increasing prices that are so burdensome that they put the business in danger of not surviving. There are strategies to consider that mitigate the risks with proactive actions. For instance, writing a narrative of the safety features of your facility and operations, being proactive in explaining any claims and reducing licensing concerns and violations for required documentation.

Property Taxes

Property taxes are a typical expense of early education business owners whether they own or lease the property. In some areas of the country, property taxes can be a significant part of the expense load. Some states allow abatement of property taxes for early education businesses, and some states have current initiatives to seek to implement property tax abatement. This reduction in expense can improve the overall financial health of a school, allowing savings to be passed along in reduced tuition, increased compensation for staff, or both. This option is a potential source of advocacy in states that are considering how to support early education programs.

Chapter 11
Mechanics and Uses of the Framework Model

In understanding the Framework Model, it is important to understand what it is, and what it is not. The model represents center-based operations with a full-time director (who could also be the owner), as well as an assistant director once a level of around sixty students is reached. The model works across all tuition rate structures, demographic groups, and sizes of schools. The model contains no owner compensation, benefits, or personal expenses unless that owner is also the director. It models a school with a market rent and fully loaded other facilities costs such as maintenance and property taxes. Knowing that every situation is unique, use the model as a guide and know that adjustments to your own financial statements may need to be made to perfectly compare actual results to the model.

Expenses are expressed as a percentage of net revenue or as a variable expense, meaning they fluctuate as net revenue changes.

There may be difficulty comparing a school that predominately accepts subsidy tuitions if those subsidies do not reflect a true market rate of the cost of care (see more information in the tuition rate chapter). Other outliers might include programs housed in a church or other facilities that don't pay rent or pay a reduced rent. Some of these programs use the expense reduction to fund lower tuition rates for parents, or higher staff wages, or a combination of both.

Others could be property tax exempt, or they could be in an older facility with lower-than-average rent and higher-than-average maintenance costs.

Whatever your situation, the model can be used as a guide.

In the model, all revenue (tuition, registration fees, late payment fees, late pickup fees, etc.) is combined into the top line revenue. Discounts are projected at 5% of revenue (staff, multiple children, industry, subsidy, etc.) and subtracted from revenue to calculate a net revenue. Net revenue is important because this should match the amount of money actually received and going into the bank. It is used as the baseline for calculating all percentages of expense categories.

What is not included: depreciation, amortization, financing costs, franchise fees, royalties, owner compensation (unless the owner is a director or teacher), owner benefits, and personal expenses.

Expenses are liberally grouped into four categories: staff costs, program costs, facility costs, and administrative costs.

Staff costs include the following: staff wages, benefits, and training. Staff wages include all pay (salary, hourly, vacation, and benefits) for all of the school's team members. Again, unless the owner is also the director or a teacher, there are no owner salaries. Benefits include health and life insurance paid by the company, retirement plans, and any other company-covered costs. Training includes any company paid costs for required training, supplemental training, outside events such as webinars and conferences, and the cost of certifications and degrees. Staff costs are benchmarked at 52-55% of net revenue at a healthy occupancy.

Program costs include the following: food, supplies, advertising, buses and vans, dues and field trips. Think of this section as everything that creates the child's day. Program costs are benchmarked at 11-14% of net revenue at a healthy occupancy.

Facility costs include the following: rent, repairs and maintenance, janitorial, lawn care, security, equipment rental, utilities, insurance, property taxes, and telephone and internet. Facility costs are benchmarked at 22-25% of net revenue at a healthy occupancy.

Administrative costs include the following: licences, bank charges, payment fees, postage, travel, contributions, and office expenses. Administrative costs are benchmarked at 1-3% of net revenue at a healthy occupancy but can be higher with more expense allocated to payment processing fees.

The tool is a useful mechanism for creating a baseline benchmark for your school. Input your school's licensed capacity and average tuition rate (for most schools the average tuition rate is the three-year-old full-time rate) and select your current occupancy. Alternatively, select an occupancy of 70%, which represents baseline financial health. Remember that the net income does not include reinvestment into your school's capital needs or growth objectives.

The model can be used to consider the impact of tuition rate increases and increased or decreased occupancy. It is a great model for determining your breakeven point in the event of negative enrollment and for having a plan to align costs quickly to secure the school's financial health.

Chapter 12
Producing Decision-Making Information

I produced financial statements that I thought were beautiful, with pages and pages of lines and figures, for directors and other decision-makers. However, I observed their glassy-eyed, confused stares as they tried to make sense of it all, so I began to break down the information that was absolutely necessary to run the business on a day-to-day basis into something more meaningful. They needed something that would allow them to quickly access information, adapt to fast changes in the business, and spend wisely, preserving resources based on their priorities. As stated previously, focusing on the Five Pillars will get you 95% of the way to financial health. Of those Five Pillars, two (occupancy and staff costs) need to be monitored every day, and three (tuition rates, discounts, and rent or mortgage costs) can be considered annually in a normalized operating environment, and at least quarterly in times of fast changing operating metrics (like the landscape since the COVID-19 pandemic began).

Information developed is a tool for decision-making rather than an administrative task to check off. It should be relevant, accurate, and timely. To be relevant, focus on the Five Pillars. To be accurate, consider outsourcing parts of your financial data if needed. Most educational business owners don't have a background in accounting, so invest in a bookkeeper or outside accounting firm to complete tasks and produce financial data as necessary. To be timely, the information must be produced quickly, with weekly information gained no later than Monday for the previous week for occupancy and salary data, and no later than ten days following the period end for monthly data. Receiving information months or even weeks after it happened is much less helpful, since you lose valuable time to adjust your strategies to preserve valuable resources that could have been spent more effectively.

Here is a list of basic information necessary to operate effectively and how to best produce each.

Weekly Monitoring

Net Revenue. Net revenue (tuition income plus other charges minus discounts) is the basis for weekly monitoring and in theory, assuming that you have collected all of your money, should be also what cash goes into the bank. It is important that you are tracking what you earned, and not just what cash went into the bank—which are two different things—as payments from families or agencies can fluctuate. This information can easily be derived from your billing system.

Occupancy. Occupancy is a measure of how well you are using your available space. Occupancy in its most accurate and useful form (see Pillar One) is net revenue divided by licensed capacity divided by average tuition rate divided by the number of periods (52 Weeks, 12 Months, or 1 Year) that the tuition rate reflects. This is your most important calculation and should be monitored weekly and strategized daily.

Salary Costs. Salary as a percentage of net revenue should be reviewed weekly for maximum control of costs and monitored daily and hourly (see Pillar Four) for maximum benefit to the school's operation. Salary costs are calculated by dividing the weekly total salary costs into the net revenue. The weekly salary costs can be gained from your payroll system.

Accounts Receivable. My hope is that this information is easy to gain and manage, because if you do nothing else, *collect the money that you earned!* Know your problems areas and follow-up on them consistently as it is the only way to stay on top of issues. Consistency and meaningful late payment fees are the key.

Every Four Weeks or Monthly Monitoring

Financial Statements. Full financial statements should be produced at minimum monthly and in your hands for review no later than ten to fifteen days following the end of the period. Personally, I'm a fan of thirteen four-week financial statements annually instead of twelve monthly statements as it can be a challenge to produce meaningful data with the complexity of calculating staff costs in the middle of a tuition week. You are constantly in the game of "there were three payroll periods in that month," or "there were five billing weeks in that month," which makes comparison and accuracy difficult. If your payroll is also monthly, then monthly financial statements are great. If not, then thirteen four-week financial statements are much more useful. The professional producing your financial statements should be able to work with this schedule and can also produce the information in whatever format that is useful to you. I am not a big fan of financial statements produced in a manufacturing format (cost of goods sold is not relevant!) for a service-based industry. I also love the Framework format that allows you to directly compare actual results to your Framework benchmark. Give your preparer the Framework model as a format and ask them to produce your reports in the format that is most meaningful for you.

Over time I have worked with many brilliant business owners who know intuitively how their company is performing. And I am in great awe of that. But moving toward more information-based analysis and using it to train the team on how financial decisions impact quality—including their own economic situations—means that you are moving closer to financial health, especially in times of quick changes.

Chapter 13
Educating Customers and Team Members

Teaching financial concepts to early education stakeholders who do not have a financial or business background has been the primary passion and focus of my career. One of my most fun projects was a class I called "Where Does All That Money Go, Anyway?" for directors and teachers. The class began by developing small teams, giving them each $100 in monopoly money, and asking them this question: for every $100 that your school earns, how much of that is spent on staff costs, program costs, facility costs, and administrative costs? I also explained what items would go in each category. Overwhelmingly the answers leaned toward huge administrative costs, with little going into staff and program costs. And oh, the arguments! At the end of the exercise, the winning team received PayDay candy bars, followed by a robust conversation about what a healthy financial structure meant to them personally in the form of raises, more PTO, benefits, more equipment and materials, and great facilities. Feel free to use this fun game with your own team!

It is also important to provide information and education to families and other decision-makers who participate in deciding how much investment to make in children's early education. I use my $45/week head-counting story often to help others understand how difficult it is for those outside the industry to understand the economics of quality early education.

The following is a communication that I share with owners as a resource to educate staff, customer stakeholders, and other decision-makers about the financial mechanics of their jobs or early education investment. I share it with you in hopes that we can spread the message about what it means to balance purpose and profit in our mission to serve families, children, and staff, and invite you to use it as a whole or in part, or edit it as you see fit, however is useful to you.

Dear "Parents," "Staff," or "Other Stakeholders":

We are honored in our partnership with you to provide children with the early care and education that they all deserve, and we are driven by this mission. There is much information in the media about the difficulties of parents paying tuition, teachers earning living wages, and schools having the resources to support both. And we agree! Staff costs have always been the largest expense for early education organizations—and for good reason. We all want early learning teachers and support staff who care for our young children to thrive in environments where they can contribute to meaningful work, advance their careers, and earn competitive wages.

The challenge for childcare owners lies in finding the right balance between competitive wages (and a rewarding work environment) and revenue derived from tuition rates. Today, this challenge is exacerbated by unprecedented increases in staff pay and the limits of what parents can afford to pay, among other factors.

We believe that in the long run, more support will be required from the government in the form of tax incentives and subsidies, in addition to from businesses that support their employees' childcare. In the meantime, if our current childcare business model breaks down, there is no care or opportunity for anyone.

As we are advocating for these systems to continue with increased support, we wanted to share some current information provided by an industry leader around the cost of care and what the typical expense load looks like in the average early education school.

Operating a business in the early education industry requires a heavy expense load, making it difficult to balance tuition rates with parent affordability. In a typical school with a healthy occupancy of 70% and above (ignoring the sharp labor cost increases currently being experienced, which are making the traditional model challenging for most providers), operating costs include the following, based on a percentage of all tuition dollars paid:

- *Staff costs such as salaries, payroll taxes, benefits, and recruiting and training at about 50-55%*
- *Program costs such as food, supplies, advertising, vehicles, and dues and licenses at approximately 12-15%*
- *Facility costs such as rent or mortgage, repairs and maintenance, janitorial, security, insurance, property taxes, utilities, and averaging 22-25%*
- *Administrative costs such as bank and ACH or credit card fees, billing systems, office supplies, travel, and internet at around 3-5%.*

This model covers the cost of operating the school and does not include any compensation for the owner, unless that owner is also a teacher or director; at 70% occupancy, these costs equate to 90% to 100% of all tuition dollars paid, leaving no resources for capital repairs, improvements, and growth. At lower occupancies, the school is likely losing cash, which is not a sustainable model. And at higher occupancies, it is possible to begin to gain the resources for reinvestment into the company and for growth.

It is our mission and purpose to create thriving environments that all children deserve, which balancing a thriving environment and economic for staff with affordability for families. Thank you for joining us in the endeavor.

What Has Become of Harriet?

Harriet came a LONG way! With a combination of maximizing enrollment, implementing a continual system of monitoring openings, increasing tuition rates to changing cost of care rates, eliminating discounts that were no longer industry norm, managing staff salaries to align with healthy metrics, and consider growth opportunities by using her landlord's resources, Harriet was ready for her second location! She was also able to take a vacation with her family this year, and for the first time since starting her company, she relaxed and enjoyed it. It's not just possible to create a business that allows children and staff to thrive—it's necessary!

Maybe that Kathy Ligon wasn't so crazy after all. . .

Part IV

Guest Chapters

The following chapters have been written and contributed by some of the industry's most amazing thought leaders. Each person has elevated early education in a unique way, sharing their talents and creativity with passion and skill. I am grateful for their individual contributions to this material and for their support of BOOST. I invite readers to get to know them better.

Chapter 14

Words Matter

By Tym Smith

Tym Smith is a valuable thought-leader in early education and a passionate advocate in elevating the recognition that educators deserve. I believe strongly in his mission to raise awareness of the critical nature of the industry and the people in it. Tym's work is grounded in care for the amazing people that make early education their life's mission.

For decades the early education industry has struggled to be recognized as a profession. The hard-working and dedicated individuals who have committed most of their lives to supporting young children and their families are amongst the lowest paid workers in the country. Despite the tremendous amount of research that supports the need for high-quality early education in children's lives both at home and while parents are working, the childcare industry continues to be belittled with the lack of recognition deserved.

The time to rewrite the script has come. Over the last five years we have finally seen a shift. Titles such as "day-care" are starting to be replaced with appropriate wording that accurately describe the work that is done. The essential needs every child needs to survive are water, food, and shelter. Professionals are starting to recognize a fourth essential need: a healthy secure attachment figure.

Traditionally, the child's attachment figure is found at home. Normally the primary person who creates a felt sense of safety needed for healthy social and emotional development is the parent. Over the past ten years, this picture has become different. Over 75% of the children in the United States are in some type of group care situation. This may be a licensed childcare program, after-school program, or Parent's Morning out. Current statistics show that 80% of these children spend more of their waking hours in these facilities than at home. Therefore, the healthy secure attachment figure becomes the classroom teacher for the majority of young children. We also know that the three most stressful events in a child's life are (1) death of a parent, (2) divorce or separation of parents and (3) a change and transition in a young child's classroom teacher. Once again, it is important to support high-quality early education programs that recognize their employees as professionals.

For those of us who have dedicated our lives to early education, being called a "day-care worker" can be triggering and insulting. Many individuals who work in a licensed child-care program ultimately leave for other employment due to a lack of recognition and the stigma that comes with inappropriate titles. However, when employees are recognized and affirmed as professionals, employees are more likely to stay and exceed expectations.

High-quality early education programs recognize that the blueprint for healthy social and emotional development is created in the early years of life. The healthy and secure care provided to these children lay the foundation for future learning and relationship building. Care is not something we do instead of teaching. Care *is* teaching!

When creating a high-quality program, early educators should build their culture, vision, and philosophy around four components.

Creating a Felt Sense of Safety

While creating and maintaining a safe physical environment is required in all programs and is needed to meet state licensing and regulatory standards, early educators must look beyond a traditional "safety checklist." Children must feel safe before they can behave in desired ways. Children must also feel safe before they can learn. A felt sense of safety must be seen from the child's point of view. Early educators must practice seeing the world from the child's version of reality.

This starts by having the secure, healthy attachment figure mentioned earlier. When a child has a perceived threat of danger or the world is not going their way, their brain is wired to search out this attachment figure. The attachment figure's presence and response wire the brain for safety. The attachment figure being available and responsive to their needs strengthens the child's ability to self-regulate.

Creating a felt sense of safety is not only needed for the children in care; it is also imperative to the adults working with these children. Just like a child, an adult must feel safe before they can meet expectations. While creating a safe workplace is required by workforce commissions and workers compensation companies, leaders who focus on building a culture where the adult also has a felt sense of safety create a professional environment with commitment, dedication, and longevity. Since 2020, the workforce crisis in the United States has provided beneficial information. Employees will leave their job when they do not feel emotional or mentally safe while at work.

Everything we do in early education should always be practiced as an adult first, child second model. Or in this perspective, a leader first, employee second model. Leaders should make it a practice every day to ensure that the working environment is safe. This starts with simple face-to-face communication. No apps, no emails, no surveys! An in-person conversation with each employee where they are asked, "Do you feel safe coming to work each day" which is followed by active listening to their verbal and nonverbal responses. (Don't forget, 77% of communication is body language and facial expressions)

Just like the relationship between the child and the adult, the leader must also be a secure healthy attachment figure for their employees.

Trust

In early education classrooms, children must trust that their caregiver is going to be there for them when they are in need. Trust is not something that is wired at birth, but must be earned and maintained. Trust requires presence. Trust requires compassion. And trust requires communication. In early education programs, 46% of relaxed alert time needs to be spent face-to-face for the first two years of life.

Studies have shown a decline in empathy over the last twenty years. We have also seen a steady decline in self-regulation for the past forty years. Empathy and self-regulation go hand-in-hand and are the key to trust. The decline in self-regulation and empathy has been tied to the lack of open-ended play in young children's lives. It is no surprise that open-ended play is needed to create trusting relationships. Many early educators make the mistake of insisting that children instantly give trust to adults. Trust must be learned. Early educators also make the mistake assuming children know how to play! Once again, play is a skill that must be taught and practice.

With the decline of empathy, self-regulation, and open-ended play, we are now seeing the newest generation of workers coming into the workforce lacking these skills. This is the first generation of workers who did not receive adequate opportunities for open-ended play. Instead, they were raised on devices such as cell phones, tablets and computers. Non-electronic play was traditionally organized sports, which is closed-ended play. Leaders of early education programs need to recognize this trend.

So, what is the best way for leaders to build trust with their employees? *Play!* Yes, play is critical for the adults in your program just as much as it is for the children. Instead of teachers watching children play, encourage the teachers to get down on the floor and play with the children. What an amazing job we have where we get paid to play! Imagine what the world would be like if everyone had this amazing opportunity—if the CEO of a Fortune 500 company took twenty minutes a day to step away from their desk or board meetings to play in a block center or string beads making fabulous patterns with their friends. Imagine how trust could look and feel different in these situations.

Connection

Healthy connections wire the brain for empathy and impulse control. When interacting and engaging with children and adults, you should focus on eye contact, presence, physical touch, and play. The need for connection never changes. There are reasons couples get divorced, and employees leave their jobs. People stop focusing on the need for meaningful connections. Every human goes through stages in their life, and depending on someone's current emotional or mental needs, their need for connection changes. Leaders and teachers should always make ongoing efforts to connect with the individuals they come into contact with.

Many people would agree that we are currently living in a world where people are disconnected. We are divided into a work of "us" and "them," where you either believe in the same thing as I do, or you're wrong. If you don't believe in the same thing I do, then you are my enemy. We also hear from early educators around the world about the changes in children's behaviors over the past five years. What has happened to connection?

Between 2020 and 2023, most of the world was wearing masks to protect themselves from the COVID-19 virus. Even today, people continue to wear a mask in environments where their health may be compromised. We did what we had to do to stay safe, healthy, and to control the virus. But we must recognize the consequences of these actions. We know from basic child development that the most fascinating object to a young child is the human face. The face gives us non-verbal cues to emotions and attachment. During the time that wearing masks was dominant, half the human face was covered for much of the time. Young children missed the opportunities and growth during this time.

Heartmath.org has also taught us that we have electromagnetic waves that travel from our heart and outward. When you have passion for something or someone, these waves travel approximately six feet from your body. Any person standing or sitting near you can feel this energy. Jon Gordon also talks about this in his book, *The Power of Positive Leadership*. Children need our presence, not our presents! The energy that comes from our bodies is essential for connection, willingness and trust. Yet, during the pandemic we were told to distance ourselves from others and to stay at least six feet away. During this time, we were not able to feel the energy of others, creating disconnect.

We also know that the human brain is wired for physical touch. Young children must have physical touch to survive. In 2020, the CDC guidelines for childcare centers recommended that infant/toddler teachers wear long sleeves to avoid physical touch on the skin. This is an example of a way that during this time, young children missed the essential importance of touch.

Lastly, during this time we had distracted adults. Parents were sent home to work. Schools closed and children were at home instead of in early education settings. Parents were forced to watch their children while also focusing on work, or in some cases, looking for work. The healthy secure attachment mentioned earlier was impacted, instead creating either anxious attachment or avoidant attachment. This had a dreadful impact on many children who were in their younger years during this time. A child's attachment style determines their ability to form relationships later in life, and many children (and adults) are still struggling to regain healthy secure attachment.

The best way to evaluate a child's attachment system is measured when the child is reunited with their adult and when they separate from adults. Many early education programs encountered mandates during the pandemic that limited parents from entering licensed childcare programs, forcing them to drop off and pick up children at the facility's front door. The reuniting and separation of adults became strained, once again damaging the social and emotional blueprint critical during this stage in life.

When you combine all these different variables, you find sources of disconnection that contributed to the lack of connection many early educators and leaders are now struggling with. The most important skill that early education programs can practice is meaningful connection, while understanding that the children are entering our programs disconnected. Employees are also reporting to work disconnected, and parents are coming in disconnected. Meaningful connection must take place every day in every interaction.

Knowing

The final component needed to create a high-quality early education program is knowing. I have worked in early education and after-school programs for over thirty years, and I strongly believe that the career is a calling. You were meant to work in early education. Most early educators and leaders enter this field as a second or third career. You arrive exactly when you were meant to arrive. You are in this industry for a reason. Many people talk about faith and belief, or even optimism. Belief can simply be defined as thoughts that you have over and over again. Knowing is an absolute. You know if your heart, you know in your mind that you were meant to be in the position you are in now. You know you got this! You know you can handle whatever challenge is in front of you. You know when you have the right employees in the right job assignments. In my opinion, nothing is more powerful that knowing!

When someone hears the words "daycare," they think of a facility warehousing children and dropping them crackers and juice a few times a day. "Daycare" is glorified babysitting. When research is published supporting the need for high-quality early education, many publications will rewrite the data and replace "early education" with words like "daycare."

People don't know what they don't know. Being an early education advocate requires us to educate people. You have the ability to rewrite the script and educate the community on who we are and why we are here. Be proud of what you do. Take the information in this chapter into consideration and reflect on your current practices. You can see we do much more than take care of a day. We care and educate young children through healthy and secure engagement. We are proud early educators.

Meet Tym

Tym Smith began working in the early education field in 1986. After spending several years in the classroom, he advanced to fill various positions including education specialist, director, and regional director. Over the past twenty years, he has spent thousands of hours training teachers and leaders across the country at local, state, and national conferences. In 2007, Tym founded Tym the Trainer, a training company dedicated to quality and diversity for early education programs. He is the owner of six early education schools in Texas and is a two-term past President of the Texas Licensed Child Care Association. Tym is a member of the Teas Trainers Registry and currently serves on the Board of Directors for the Association for Early Learning Leaders. He is a Conscious Discipline certified instructor, a Jon Gordon certified instructor, and a certified Life is Good Playmaker.

Tym can be reached at tym@tymthetrainer.com

Resources

Bailey, R. A. (2011). Managing emotional mayhem: The five steps for self-regulation. Loving Guidance.

HeartMath Institute. www.heartmath.org

"Attachment Theory" founded by John Bowlby, expanded by Mary Ainsworth and adapted by Dir. Becky Baily and Conscious Discipline.

The Council for Professional Recognition. *Essential for Working with Young Children.*

Chapter 15

Marketing Strategies for Enrollment Success

By Kathe Petchel

Kathe Petchel is a passionate and enthusiastic trainer focusing on business concepts for early education business owners with a specialty focus on strategies for building strong teams. In addition, she owns three early education centers in Virginia where she practices what she preaches!

In the ever-evolving childcare landscape, the refrain 'out with the old, in with the new' resonates as childcare centers navigate complexities, including those that have arisen due to the COVID-19 pandemic. What marketing strategies will serve us well going forward, and which ones should be discontinued? The solution is an interesting puzzle with complicated elements we need to balance. On the surface is the obvious need to stabilize our childcare organizations to protect them from future challenges including competitors, regulators at both the federal and state levels, funding sources, interest rates, and overall political and financial uncertainty. An ideal solution will be versatile and malleable, and able to be customized for various challenges. At the core, however, is the formidable hiring challenge that highlights the need to fully restructure our HR systems beginning with recruiting and hiring, enhancing onboarding and initial training, and robust mentoring professional development.

The combination of financial insecurity driven by the loss of grants and other funding, along with social unrest and technological innovations, has profoundly reshaped the landscape of childcare organizations worldwide. The tumultuous waves of recent social change driven by movements advocating racial justice, gender equality, and economic equity have prompted many childcare organizations to consider reassessing and reinventing from the ground up. After acknowledging the need for change, highlighted largely by the challenge of successfully hiring and retaining childcare staff, it appears that new systems are emerging designed to more effectively develop the next generation of early education leaders. Initiatives such as online training platforms complete with personal videos, targeted assessments and activities, opportunities for virtual childcare certifications and advanced degrees, and extending the length of training are strategies that serve both employees and families. When faced with enrollment waitlists due to a lack of qualified teachers, high absenteeism, and high turnover, solving the problem of staffing must be blended with marketing for enrollment strategies.

Due to an exhausted and challenging workforce that is complicated by the addition of an inexperienced Generation Z, experienced teachers choosing early retirement, and mass resignations of childcare employees, creative and positive messaging is essential as we seek to serve young children and their families successfully. In this era of digital dominance, unpredictable consumer behavior, economic instability, and an uncertain political climate, the key to successful marketing lies in embracing innovation. Early childhood leaders would be well-served to become competent with new technology and leverage emerging modern marketing techniques. The transformative power of modern marketing techniques tailored specifically for childcare centers will usher in a new era of growth, ensure relevance, and support sustainability while fostering greater family support and engagement.

Certainly, we need to continue powerful employment practices, such as modelling relationship-building techniques and effective problem-solving, that will help us nurture and lead our teams. It's also necessary to provide education and opportunities to explore emotional intelligence and effective listening. Our organizations will benefit from becoming more comfortable with uncomfortable moments, expecting challenges from upset colleagues and parents, and developing strategies to support children needing assistance with emotional regulation. Having the insight and ability to take a breath and pause before responding represents highly desirable social skills that lead to enrollment success and staff retention. Looking at all aspects of our program, including the staffing and technology pieces, will support the new foundation necessary for the future. Marketing staff benefits, training opportunities, and initiatives to support children's current needs will lead to enrollment success. Educating parents about these efforts, particularly around staff support, will enhance enrollment efforts and enhance family retention. Families desire childcare stability and a program with successful operations, long-term commitment, and stable staff. Parents will stay away from unstable programs, fearing they may close.

Make no mistake: no money, no mission. In the childcare world, margins are tight, and only by managing a multitude of shifting variables will a program succeed profitably. Keeping a close eye on HINGE's Five Pillars and taking one at a time ensures most programs will experience significant improvement and eventually profitability. The current parent consumers we serve are largely Millennials and Generation Z, so understanding their decision-making processes and individual and family needs demands that we adapt our marketing roles and strategies. How particular generations make buying decisions, including childcare, relates to their life experiences, career and parenting goals, and financial acumen.

Generation Z—also known as Zoomers—(born 1997-2012) is emerging as a unique group of employees and parent consumers who have arguably been the most impacted by the pandemic. Not only did many experience interruptions to their educations, but they also missed many cultural coming of age moments such as graduations, prom, birthdays, travel, sports banquets, and other celebrations, as well as the loss or limitation of emotionally significant milestone events such as weddings, funerals, and the birth of babies.

From a workforce point of view, during the pandemic they missed typical opportunities to learn in high school and college and were instead permitted relaxed testing requirements and limited or non-existent in-person learning. Many weren't able to join the workforce or had to work remotely, resulting in different and usually more lenient expectations from their employers. Generation Z largely was restricted to their homes, reducing their social interaction and therefore their social maturity and experiences. They widely report that they experience challenges with mental health, including anxiety and depression, and fear suicide for themselves and others, as well as mass shootings. Unfortunately, many report getting medical and mental health advice from platforms like TikTok and unqualified sources. It's no surprise that employers are frustrated and discouraged with Generation Z. We have a lot of catching up to do before we can fully count on them as young leaders.

On the other hand, Gen Z is incredibly resilient, creative, and confident. They are considered digital natives—the first social generation to have grown up with full access to the internet, social media, and portable digital technology, including smartphones from a young age. They have a short attention span, can maneuver multiple digital platforms and devices at once, and consume hundreds of texts and digital information a day. It's important to understand that the old rules of digital marketing that work with Millennials increasingly don't apply to Gen Z.

In terms of their spending habits, they're quite the opposite of millennials. Generation Z tends to save money, enjoy thrifting, and uphold frugal habits. Like Millennials, they make it a point to purchase from companies that reflect their values. Many still live at home with their parents or other relatives, meaning less of their money is tied up on larger expenses such as rent, groceries, and utilities. In a 2021 Bloomberg report, Generation Z collectively had 360 billion dollars in disposable income.

A November 2022 survey found almost 40 percent of Gen Z in the U.S. spend more than four hours on social media platforms daily, with many reporting much more than that. Also, in 2022 research found the average Gen Z user in the U.S. spent over 1,500 minutes watching YouTube content monthly. (Statista, March 2024, Dixon, S.J). Their favorite social platforms are YouTube, Instagram, TikTok, and Snapchat. A large percentage report they regularly purchase items they see on social media. Some aspire to be TikTok or Instagram influencers and follow many influencers avidly. They are less worried about furthering their education, despite their parents' encouragement, because they have been inspired by successful social media influencers. They also realize that they can easily improve their education virtually, with many customized options available online.

Understanding the relationship between our hiring challenges and our enroll-ment goals is essential for enrollment success, which leads to sustainable quality programs and consistent profitability. Gone are the days when one marketing strategy can be counted on. Utilizing multiple opportunities to educate parent consumers about our programs via their desired social media channels, along with consistent word-of-mouth referrals and a steady stream of positive reviews and testimonials delivered in short bites, ideally across multiple platforms, works!

While selecting childcare is quite different than choosing other consumer goods, there are several effective marketing strategies to engage a Zoomer customer:

1. Since Generation Z is swift and savvy on social media, use social media trends to your advantage. Utilize your Generation Z staff or parents to stay informed about current viral content and in-the-moment trends seen on TikTok, Reels, or YouTube shorts and mimic using popular phrases or memes. Keep it simple and engaging. Better yet, have a Gen Z-er create it for you. No need to be perfect, just engaging. This strategy works for both hiring and enrolling. For example, using a Taylor Swift meme or content related to her will likely reap engagement.

2. Since 68% of Gen Z conduct online searches several times a day, be sure you have optimized your Google business profile, as well as Google Maps. Since 65% of Gen Z-ers want to travel ten miles or less to do business, pay special attention to local engagement and targeted ads within ten miles of your business. Additionally, consider geofencing for the same purpose.

3. You must be responsive when the phone rings or you receive a text or email because Generation Z has very little tolerance for a lack of speedy responses. The phone should be answered within three rings and texts and emails responded to immediately. It's a good idea to allow multiple well-trained staff to support this including in the evenings and weekends, especially if you need to increase enrollment quickly.

4. Authenticity and originality matter more to Generation Z than beautiful-ly curated content. This means the expectation of a beautiful Instagram aesthetic is unnecessary for Gen Z who favor an earthier aesthetic. Since they will likely research your company in multiple ways, the goal is to capture their attention, so they continue the research. Being relatable is the first step to being known, liked, and trusted.

Don't be surprised if grandparents are heavily involved in Generation Z's decisions regarding childcare. Use this opportunity to embrace them to mutually support Generation Z and their Alpha generation children (born 2013-present). Generation Z's parents are likely Generation X, who are presently in the high-earning and growth stages of their careers. They may be financially supporting Generation Z as well as undertaking responsibility for elderly family members.

Like all generations, Millennials (born 1981-1996) have particular traits related to their life experiences as a group, how they were parented and educated, as well as their unique challenges and opportunities during the pandemic. As a parent consumer group, Millennials care deeply about the overall mission and value of a company and, once they have bought in, are likely to be loyal and supportive. From an enrollment point of view, they value understanding the mission and core values of the company before enrolling. However, should they find the preschool neglects to follow its stated mission and values and does not correct issues quickly, they will readily voice their dissatisfaction to their social media contacts, neighborhood friends, and work colleagues.

Many Millennials have Baby Boomers as parents. Baby Boomers are highly driven for success, not just at work but with their parenting and child-rearing goals and want more than anything the best life could offer their children. Many traditional Baby Boomers believed that education, including college, would ensure their children would be successful and sacrificed to provide them with this opportunity. Baby Boomers, in possibly a misguided effort to be sure their Millennial children succeeded, became overly competitive, 'helicopter' parents and in many cases protected their children from disappointment by awarding participation trophies and gold stars for effort. This left Millennials a bit surprised when college professors and employers demanded efforts and rewards for quality work. Now, as adults, Millennials view the older generations as overly work-obsessed and have adopted a more relaxed view of work as well as child-raising and parenting. This corresponds with the popularity of play-based, Montessori, and Reggio-type programs vs. the traditional academic style kindergarten prep philosophy. Since Millennials as a group felt pushed towards achievement, they resist pushing their young children towards academic achievement, understanding the anxiety and frustration they may have experienced.

Effective Strategies to Serve Millennial Parent Consumers

1. Educate on current early childhood research and focus on the value of play-based learning, curiosity, and the wonder of childhood. This will resonate with Millennials and start a great conversation.
2. Instill confidence that learning truly takes place when children explore their world and show growth through sample portfolios, well-thought-out parent conferences, and regular parent education.
3. Increase school community activities to allow parents opportunities to connect with peers, particularly since some are still working remotely. Consider that parents likely don't live near their family of origin and would welcome opportunities for connections and guidance.
4. Use your school environment, especially the classroom setup, as the third teacher, and ensure the classroom is an inviting environment.
5. Emphasize the value of outdoor classrooms and educate on the concept of risk vs. hazard in play. This makes sense to Millennials, particularly ones who may have been overly protected by those helicopter (or sometimes snowplow) parents.

Like Generation Z, Millennials care greatly about the environment, so adding organic gardens, water testing to ensure safe drinking, and Green certifications including reducing toxins will be appreciated.

Marketing strategies vary depending on factors such as the local market, family demographics, kindergarten entrance standards, and the number of enrollment spaces available in a given area. Birth rates and projected growth in a community must be considered, particularly to plan for a sustainable and financially healthy program. The competitive landscape may dictate, to some extent, the level of marketing and advertising investment a program must make to secure full enrollment. In general, having a comprehensive and flexible marketing plan is essential to be fully prepared. Lack of preparation may mean the loss of enrollment opportunities, especially if you are in an area or operate a program that suffers from high staff turnover or challenges with staff recruiting. Under almost no circumstances should you stop touring your school unless your waitlist is verified and you are confident there will be no spaces for the foreseeable future. In that case, please consider taking a good look at your tuition rates, as they likely should be increased. By touring, you have the opportunity to build goodwill, develop relationships with future families, and let families know when you expect to have a space. You'll absolutely want staff hired and trained before opening a new classroom, but by not touring a family, you guarantee they will go elsewhere. In my experience, openings arise at any time, and you want to be first to build enrollment with your desired customers.

Additional financial factors such as the level of local, state, or federal funding, corporate partnership opportunities, and the ability to successfully negotiate financial terms for various creative growth opportunities may be significant.

Regardless of these nuances, there are marketing and enrollment strategies that work well in almost all situations because parents universally want what is best for their children. Savvy programs aim to deliver this by articulating their why and explaining what makes their program special and unique. Most parents will sacrifice financially, drive farther, and accommodate scheduling conflicts if the level of quality care is consistent and their child is happy and thriving.

Consider your program goals and your ability to execute the action steps necessary to succeed. Make your plan and build your marketing team starting with your teachers and parents! Excellent word-of-mouth is not only the foundation necessary to grow enrollment but the easiest and least expensive. Providing high-quality activities with enthusiastic teachers who can nurture both children and parents is the foundation of your marketing plan. Once you have this element in place, look for other opportunities to serve and love your school community.

Instead of simply listing basic marketing 101–type ideas, I want to encourage marketing based on traits I find that childcare professionals embody. I welcome you to look over the following positive and actionable adjectives as inspiration and then, together with your team, create a customized marketing plan with a timeline, specific goals, and deadlines and designate team members to execute. Hold them accountable with fun contests or gamify the project. Be willing to pivot if something truly doesn't work but be patient as you implement new initiatives since marketing success may take time.

Be Authentic

Create short videos or reels to post on social media illustrating the joy in our work. Include videos of teachers in particular age groups and highlight their unique strengths and skills. For example, a bilingual teacher may teach Spanish or Russian in the classroom! Create a video of the activity or lesson, even if it's as simple as reading a familiar book (perhaps *Chick Chicka Boom Boom* in their native language). Not only will you be promoting an additional curriculum feature, but parents and potential team members will be able to picture themselves or their children in this classroom!

Be Creative

One of the best parts of early childhood entrepreneurship is creating a business based on your dreams and personal mission. Using your creative energy when marketing or promoting your brand makes your company stand out. For example, perhaps you have a fun way to answer the phone, a particular tour gift, or unusual event. Make it your goal to showcase your program's differences. Another way to say this is "zig when they zag." Rather than doing what your competitors do, think way outside the box and do something different!

- Do a crazy family field trip event. Rent a bus and go to a baseball game, a theme park, or a nature area, and get to know each other.
- Have a team goal with your staff and reward them with an unexpected gesture—a day off with pay, a generous gift card, a shopping spree or lunch on you! Really, they'll love it. A popular team reward is a team trip!
- I have my team toss beach balls (branded, of course) over all the local pool fences over the Memorial Day weekend. Who doesn't want to play with beach balls?

Be Organized

Create a marketing plan that you and your team can execute. As Stephen Covey suggests, "Begin with the end in mind." Without a roadmap of your enrollment (or hiring) goals, you'll have trouble tracking progress. Marketing plans can be easily adapted and analyzed when you track each element. It's easy to delegate specific parts of the marketing plan to team members or to outsource when you have a high-level view.

Be Confident

Stand firm with two feet in the ground regarding your enrollment (and other) policies. Making exceptions sets you up for confusion and possibly angry parents. Be careful not to favor any client or family. Don't lower your standards to get the enrollment. For example, a parent may ask for a discount or extended hours beyond your current operating schedule. Resist the urge to accommodate since favoritism usually becomes an issue.

Be Kind

Listen patiently before responding to frustrated parents or tired and emotional staff. For many parents, this may be their first time with a preschooler at school all day. There may be a bit of guilt at leaving their little one, and while they may come across as confident, they may need help expressing their expectations and concerns. We all fumble a bit. Asking open-ended questions is a great start. Welcome concerns and immediately address issues. My team has a goal of responding within one hour. The problem may not be completely solved, but the frustration will be minimized since the person will feel they are a priority. Be clear about your plan to correct anything necessary going forward. Being thankful for the opportunity to have a conversation that will help the parent continue to come to you with concerns in the future. Welcoming future communication opportunities will go a long way toward clearing the air and rebuilding trust.

Be Flexible

Hold tours and open houses. If you are in an area where families move frequently, such as a university town or military base, offer virtual tours.

Be Thoughtful

Show appreciation for referrals and send a handwritten thank you and a small gift. People love receiving surprises in the mail, especially children after a tour. Consider touches such as placing colorful confetti in the envelope for fun.

Be Strategic

Do the math—strategize and play with your tuition rates for the best enrollment opportunities. What serves your goals better? Enrolling five-day full-time children, or offering part-time care at a higher rate to fill slots more quickly? Investing in an outdoor classroom or completing deferred maintenance? Know the growth opportunities in your area—be thoughtful with outreach to local builders and model homes. Go armed with enrollment and hiring flyers. Regularly pop by with thank-you treats. Anytime you can plan a win-win partnership with community members you will build your brand and reputation.

Be Honest

Let parents know exactly when you will raise rates each year and give plenty of warning. When a teacher leaves, even if unexpected, be transparent about your plan to replace the teacher including information about how families can refer potential staff to you. Best practice: thank parents for staff referrals with a generous gift or tuition credit.

Be Proactive

Ask for feedback from parents and staff. Use Survey Monkey or create a simple Google or Jot form with no more than ten questions. Be sure some of them are open-ended to get the most ideas and clarity. Ideally, the surveys require their name so you can address them effectively. However, if you run into a school culture issue, or a gaggle of grumpy parents or staff, you may want to have anonymous surveys because the most important element is honest feedback. You could set an expectation of civility by asking recipients to please word the feedback and suggestions as positively and kindly as possible. Receiving feedback is a great way to improve quickly and get your finger on the school's pulse. I've learned that if one person asks or complains, others likely have the same concerns. Wouldn't you rather someone allow you to correct an error or explain a policy than create a negative post on social media or disenroll their child? The lifetime value of a customer is enormous in our industry, and being proactive about feedback is an inexpensive, though sometimes uncomfortable, means to correct a problem.

Be Brave

Ask for parent testimonials and referrals, especially if a parent gives a compliment about an event, a classroom, or a teacher. Most parents are happy to promote your program at work, on social media, or at the bus stop! Reciprocating with a thank you note, promo item, or small gift will further build the relationship.

After thanking them for a positive comment, immediately ask them if they mind sharing the compliment on a particular platform. Choose the platform based on the current reviews or the platform you'd like to improve. Be careful not to overdo it on a particular platform by asking for too many reviews at once. It's better to have a steady drip of positive testimonials (for all your locations and age groups) than to run a testimonial contest and have them all posted at once. Why? The pesky internet SEOs will catch on and think these aren't authentic testimonials and you may be penalized by having the posts deleted or worse, be blocked from the platform. Consider testimonials and reviews for the following: Facebook, Google Business, Yelp, Twitter (X) and childcare platforms such as care.com and winnie.com

Be Active

Engaging on various social media platforms is an easy and inexpensive way to promote your program creatively. Your locations should have Facebook, Instagram, Pinterest, Twitter (X) accounts, and it is ideal to engage with your audience daily. This is an excellent opportunity for a Millennial or Generation Z staff member to contribute.

Be Happy

Early childhood should be a joyful time, and the adults working with young children should have an upbeat attitude. Our shared goals include providing safe environments, engaging children in active learning, and educating children to be socially confident with values that reflect well on their families and our schools. Creating school communities requires effort and choosing staff with positive and happy energy will help attract more of the same. However, our teams look to their leaders for inspiration and modeling. Be happy!

Be Techy

ChatGPT is one of many great modern tools for creating and editing content and inspiring ideas. The app is easy to use, and most download it on their phone. Utilize it as a handy tool for daily communication, newsletters, educational content, and outreach. Give the app specific and clear instructions and then edit away! Be sure to ask for more examples and tweak your feedback with specific edits. Know your voice and ask ChatGPT to create content in your voice. For example: nurturing, professional, family-oriented, positive, supportive, kind. You can also ask ChatGPT to gear content to Millennial moms, Baby Boomer retirees, Gen Z, etc.

Of course, what works for one program may not be the best solution for another, but your willingness to set a goal, make a plan, and execute the necessary steps will start you on the road to success. As always, offering your team the opportunity to grow and develop their skills will help you build leaders and enrollment. Utilizing parent and community support will get you where you want to be faster.

Meet Kathe

Kathe Petchel has worked in early childhood education since 1980. After teaching kindergarten and first grade, she opened her first childcare center in 1984. She is a multi-site childcare owner with three preschools in Charlottesville, Virginia serving more than 400 families. Kathe joined HINGE in 2017 and is currently a member of the Business Development team. Kathe is a regular speaker at national and international conferences creating presentations related to current early education innovations, operations best practices, exit strategies, and succession planning. Working closely with state childcare associations, Kathe has a strong interest in supporting fellow owners.

Kathe can be reached at kpetchel@hingeadvisors.com.

Chapter 16
The Importance of Branding
By Neel Sengupta

Neel Sengupta has developed a strong team of professionals at Better Beans Branding that focuses on branding for the early education industry. Branding (so much more than colors and logos!) is an important concept in driving the enrollment of a school and in communicating the value of its services. Their work has elevated the professionalism of schools across the country.

Introduction: Intentional Branding Gets the Job Done. Anything Less is for Losers.

The goal of this chapter is to provide a brief, clear overview for how to impact your brand and how the impact and method you take can pay massive dividends for your business. Branding is winning.

We'll explore:

- Comprehensive approach to branding
- Emphasize the tangible advantages of branding and remodeling your schools
- Analyze the return on investment of a branding effort
- Discuss the process of auditing your school's impact on all five senses

- Uncover some insights that major operators understand but often struggle to implement as swiftly as you can.

If you've previously attended any one of HINGE's events, SHIFT, or Thrive, you'll know that Kathy has consistently emphasized the importance that brand evolution and facility design can have on business valuation. For readers of this chapter who don't know Better Beans Branding, what we share here isn't theory. It is applied guidance and expertise tested over hundreds of clients and businesses across multiple industries.

Kathy and the HINGE team have been both clients and cheerleaders for Better Beans. Year after year, Kathy's annual report on the state of the industry regularly includes branding as a key action item for improving the financial health of your business.

Further, she says it is vital to commanding the highest price for your business at the time of sale because it gets the attention of savvy buyers who have greater confidence in what they buy because of the intentionality of your branding efforts and results. Let that sink in—if your exit strategy is to identify the best buyer for your business so that your legacy can continue to grow and develop, you may well be best served by developing tactics that ensure your business stands out to those buyers.

Our work at Better Beans began initially as a process implemented for our own preschool operations (under another name) years before the launch of our branding company. You may read about this experience in the chapter contributed by Thad Joiner, Better Beans CEO and formerly CEO of Sunbrook Academy and Co-Founder of Cedars Preschools, both brands now operated by private equity groups.

The Limited View: Old Branding

As we look at the impact of your brand, it is important to consider a full viewpoint. To do that we first have to understand the limited but still dominant view across the industry: your brand is your visual identity, and that identity is your logo. Period. Savvy operators have extended well beyond the limited view to include how the logo and general aesthetics are used with external marketing, particularly how your company presents itself on your website, or social media.

We know and agree that this is important, but it's still limited. It is not complete, not by a long shot.

At Better Beans we believe a more developed viewpoint is that your brand is the experience your customer has or may have with your business. From that viewpoint, you can see that your brand isn't simply a printed or produced visual identity, or your website or social media presence—it is more. You can influence the experience of course through quality operations, but what about other attributes?

Better Beans considers the brand as an expression of your vision, story, and unique attributes and benefits. Your company has the opportunity to translate your vision and these messages into an experience for your customers and staff, who will reward your business with loyalty, referrals, support and ultimately repeat business. We believe your brand experience starts in your parking lot and extends throughout your physical space inside and outside of your building.

Our work positions your brand to tell your story through physical attributes of interior design (by remodel and built out school spaces), exterior building and curb appeal, playground creation, and quality signage.

What's the Opportunity? Brand Experience is Tangible Value

The opportunity with brand development and communicating the brand experience particularly with physical change to your space and messaging is that when we do it successfully, we have either kept up with the Joneses, or better yet, replaced the Joneses. Either way, new and improved can last a long time in retail, and the ROI on this is measurable. You'll note that most successful franchise operators outside the childcare industry typically go through some form of physical evolution of their customer experience space, such as a remodel, every six to seven years.

The tangible value of an evolving customer experience through brand development is typically one or more of the following:

1. **Increased Tuition Rates:** Why? Because your intentional development is designed to provide improved customer experiences. Kathy regularly says if you aren't planning your price increases to account for improving your business, then you are missing out.

2. **Increased Loyalty:** Why? When owners and directors communicate their "reasons why" and their "expertise how," they are aligning their company with reasons to be patronized. They are clear and concise with their benefits to the customer, and the customer can easily differentiate them from competitors. This results in retention and loyalty. We like to say to show them why you want them more and what they get for being your patron. The sale doesn't stop when they enroll.

3. **Increased Enrollments:** Why? Well-designed spaces (inside and out) along with intentional, impactful signage and reliable consistent operations result in improvement in conversions of tours to enrollments. Simply put, old-dated daycares are not competitive with beautiful preschools. Enrollments happen because families see the investment. Read on later about the dangers of "limping in."

4. **Improved Staff Morale and Retention:** Why? When staff feel great about their workspace and can recognize the investment a company and its leaders are making in the environment, they, in turn, show up and do inspired work. Happy teachers contribute to successful businesses. Their morale and their subconscious willingness to be a part of your change forward cuts down on attendance issues and raises the standard of performance. Essentially, they reengage the team and feel a part of something bigger than themselves. As an added benefit, you can leverage this into recruiting others in the community looking to work in a freshly designed and remodeled school.

Addressing Five Senses Through Facility Experience

Given the viewpoint that your brand is an experience, it's important to consider how customers and prospective customers engage the experience. We suggest that a great starting point for that engagement is to consider the five senses. Our prospective families get the best from you when you are clear and intentionally communicating. That means intentionally addressing how your school smells, looks, feels (touch), sounds, and even tastes.

We recommend an unbiased walk through your school. Conduct your own audit, and then when you are done, go to a couple of your competitors and secret shop them. In fact, go to your best competitor. Ask yourself what these experiences are yielding for your and their customers. Here are a few ways to view your school and consider the five senses as a part of the experience.

Feel free to email us at info@betterbeansbranding.com and we will send you a complimentary Top 10 Keys to A Successful Audit of Your School.

Example 1: Parking lot

- **Sight:** Is it clean? How is the surfacing? Is the striping presentable for parking? Is the landscape around the lot in order?
- **Sound:** Does it creak and crumble below your car? Can you hear it?
- **Smell:** Do you smell oil leaks from cars or feral cat pee? Do you smell anything positive?
- **Touch/Feel:** Perhaps here you consider functionality. Is there enough parking for your clients' needs? Is there action necessary to improve the parking lot? If yes, what?

Example 2: Lobby

- **Sight:** Clean and clutter free? Is the entrance presentable? Is there a sign in or near the lobby that lets you know whether you've entered a highly reputable school or a mom-and-pop daycare?
- **Sound:** What do you hear when you enter? Are you greeted? Is there background music? How does the staff answer the phone, meaning what does that sound like? Do they sound professional?
- **Touch/Feel:** Are there tactile experiences for children in the lobby? Does the lobby have a space for meeting the director or other business leaders? Do the materials in the lobby's buildout appear to be appropriate for childcare operations? Are the lobby's touchpoints and customer interaction areas comfortable to do business in? Is the space used effectively?
- **Taste:** Does the lobby offer any amenities such as coffee, water, or snacks for touring families? Did your tour include an opportunity to taste today's lunch? Or snack? Was it easy to understand the meal program and nutrition offerings at the school?

- **Smell**: Does the lobby smell fresh and inviting, or musty, old and dated? Do you smell diapering beyond the doors? How about cooking smells from today's broccoli with cheese sauce? Does the school invest in a scent program?

What the Big Companies Know, but Won't Do, That You Can and Should

Large childcare operators understand the importance of presenting a cohesive brand across their system. They recognize that the brand encompasses the entire customer experience, including interactions within school spaces such as lobbies, classrooms, playgrounds, and parking lots. However, their scale makes it impractical to invest significant sums into every single location simultaneously. For instance, if the average remodel costs $250,000, a private equity group with 100 locations would require $25 million in additional investment to implement brand evolution system-wide simultaneously. Note, I'm not saying a remodel effort is $250k; this is just for illustration purposes.

Instead, big companies adopt a precise and formulaic approach to where and how they invest in branding and remodeling, which often results in slower decision-making processes.

This presents an opportunity for smaller regional brands or single-site operators competing against established national chains. By outspending their competition on branding and messaging, these smaller operators can force larger companies to follow rather than lead.

Consider the potential return on investment (ROI) of a significant remodel and rebranding effort. If signage, interior, and exterior remodeling cost $500,000, the following considerations can help understand the ROI:

- **Increased Enrollment:** A shiny, new facility could attract twenty-five new students within six months, generating $250,000 in additional annual revenue. That's a two-year window to recover the cost of a remodel and a lasting increase in top line revenue and bottom-line profits.
- **Expanded Capacity:** A remodel could address changing the capacity of a school, increasing opportunity beyond the current licensing capacity. If you could add to classroom counts, wouldn't you take it if it fits within

your operation? A classroom expansion of twenty-five students is truly added revenue above the former capacity.

- **Tuition Increase:** A 10% increase in tuition across the board for 150 students could result in an extra $150,000 in revenue during the remodel year alone. Making a tuition increase align with a remodel ensures that families equate improvement in their school to your fee structure.

In addition to these financial benefits, a remodel and intentional rebranding effort can also enhance the real estate value of the school property and increase the overall sale value of the business. Consulting with experts like Kathy and the HINGE team can provide further insights into the value of branding as a sound investment.

So, you can see the value of a remodel and that intentional rebrand pays for itself, to say nothing of impacting the real estate value of your school property and the sale value of your business. Ask Kathy and the HINGE team to weigh in on this. Ultimately, branding is a sound investment.

Never Stop Telling Your Story

There's a marketing saying that goes something like this: "There's not one way to get a thousand customers, but there are a thousand ways to get one." I'd love to give credit to whomever said it, but I know I've heard it over a dozen times. Brand story telling is a key driver of customer acquisition even one at a time. Eventually telling the story repeatedly turns into a listening audience of many.

In this age of low attention span, highly competitive and costly advertising, increased demand for your services, and more competition, you have to tell your story well, consistently, and frequently.

Continuously share your brand narrative. Master your story and adeptly tailor it to various contexts and diverse audiences. Equip your leaders, directors, and especially your sales team with this skill. Encourage practice and role-play sessions to refine storytelling abilities. Learning how to articulate your school's story and its unique appeal effectively will transform prospects into buyers, and buyers into fervent believers who become advocates for your brand. While there's no single formula for attracting and retaining customers, consistently recounting your story with freshness and enthusiasm is paramount. Repetition is key; never tire of sharing your narrative as if it's the first time you're telling it and the first time someone is hearing it. Frequency reinforces connection.

Signage

At Better Beans, we prioritize effective storytelling, and a crucial aspect of this is crafting clear, well-produced signage that highlights the unique advantages for both prospective families and staff. To enhance your school's appeal, ensure you have three to five engaging tour stops that showcase the distinct benefits of joining your school community. Avoid recycling generic information commonly touted by competitors. Instead, focus on what sets your school apart. If that's curriculum, then show how it uniquely fosters student success and how it leads to tangible student achievements.

Bonus: A Common Mistake… Limping in is for Brand Losers

We live in a time where there's a significant triumph of home renovation shows. You can easily list three or four different ones on any given night of the week. The success of HGTV and its influence is obvious. You've likely heard show hosts eagerly declare, "Are you ready to see your dream home?" or "Move that bus!" These enthusiastic proclamations wouldn't carry weight if the show didn't deliver substantial, visible transformations. In contrast, you don't hear a host say, "Are you ready to see the two rooms we painted?" Consider this: as a viewer, you're captivated and impressed by significant, tangible changes. The same principle applies to your customers and community. Half-hearted efforts won't earn your business the recognition it deserves for the investment in change. We advocate for identifying areas for improvement and diving in wholeheartedly. Don't merely dress up a lackluster situation and expect remarkable results—lipstick on a pig generally won't win the beauty pageant.

Meet Neel

Neel Sengupta is COO and Managing Partner at Better Beans Branding. He has a passion for helping business owners realize their vision through intentional design and seeing the impact this can make on workplaces and people. Neel lives in Atlanta, is married, and a father of two girls. In his spare time, he is working on learning to fish and play golf.

Neel can be reached at neel@betterbeansbranding.com.

Chapter 17

Recruiting, Growing, and Retaining an Excellent Team

By Aleta Mechtel

Aleta Mechtel is a passionate creator of solutions for staffing early education schools with the development of a substitute teacher organizations whose mission is to fill capacity with highly qualified substitute teachers. She is the former owner of four schools in Minneapolis and the HINGE team is proud to have been a part of her transition out of her operating early education centers so that she could continue her work in solving the staffing crisis!

In the industry of childcare, each new hire becomes a part of the success of every family, child, and other employee in your center. The impact of the individuals hired to take on the roles and responsibilities in your classrooms cannot be overstated. This chapter will review the entire process of making sure that you have the best strategies in place for recruiting, building, and retaining a high performing team. Building this team will be the foundation for running and growing an exceptional childcare center.

The goal of this information is to ensure you hire the right individuals to nurture the growth, development, and happiness of every child who attends your childcare center. Whether you are an experienced, long-term childcare owner or getting ready to open your first center, the information in this chapter will help you onboard a team that not only meets but exceeds the needs of your company.

Birth through five years of age is a critical time of discovery, development, and growth. The impact of a dedicated, skilled, and compassionate team expands far beyond the walls of your center, reaching into the homes, schools, and communities you serve. The employees you bring on board will create the strongest foundation for every child's life that becomes a part of your center.

Before you do any recruiting, you need to determine what the specific needs of your childcare center staffing needs are. By identifying roles, responsibilities, and the unique demands of your company, you need to create clear expectations and assemble a team that can seamlessly integrate into your educational philosophy, core values, vision, and mission. Creating clear job descriptions becomes the next crucial step, as we fulfill the competencies, qualifications, and the customer service approach necessary for success.

Specific strategies and processes need to be created for recruitment, interviewing, onboarding, training, and retention. All are essential components in building a positive team culture that contributes to the overall success of your center.

My hopes for you are that when you read this chapter, you will be able to hire the right people for your childcare center to experience low turnover. My goal is for your team to not only meet but also exceed expectations of the children and families you serve.

Identifying Your School's Needs

The initial step of building your team is to really understand the employment needs of your center. Identifying these needs is not a one-size-fits-all attempt but a hire that will align with your center's core values, goals, and the needs of the children you aim to serve.

Begin by assessing your staffing requirements based on capacity, ratios, age groups, and any special job roles to fulfill what your program needs, such as cooks, bus drivers, janitors, etc.

Make sure to define roles and responsibilities clearly. Create the different roles within your center, such as directors, assistant directors, teachers, assistants, etc., and outline the specific tasks associated with each. This not only gives you clarity for effective recruitment but also establishes a solid foundation for teamwork and collaboration among staff members.

By taking the time to identify your center's needs, you are creating a successful hiring process that is strategic, purposeful, and aligned with the mission of your childcare center. This important step sets the stage for creating effective job descriptions and strategies for successful recruitment.

Writing a Clear Job Description

Writing a clear job description is a step-by-step roadmap of expectations for anyone who works for you. Make sure to review it often so it is always up to date and accurate. You will refer to this in any onboarding, training, and reviews. It will also help you create the outline for you to build your processes for each area of the employee's responsibilities. A well-written, clear job description not only attracts the right candidates but also serves as clarification for the roles and responsibilities expected within your center. Once this is completed, post this job description everywhere you can think of, including your company website, your personal social media, Facebook groups, Indeed, and college job boards. Email your team and families and invite your team and families to share on their social media platforms.

A clear job description template should include:
- Branding
- Job Title/Position
- Age Level
- Who They Report To
- Job Type: Full Time, Part Time, Salary or Hourly
- Overview of Position
- Responsibilities (Tasks Associated with This Role)

The Interview Process

The interview process is the next step in building an excellent team for your childcare center. Thoroughly reviewing your applicants will help you find out their qualifications, experience, and most importantly, their alignment with your company's core values. You want to create an experience for these applicants as you are interviewing them. Screen your applicants, filtering through who has applied to assess whether they are the right fit for your center and your center is a right fit for them. Childcare is not for everyone. When hiring times are tough and finding people is difficult, make sure that you are not taking warm bodies to fill your vacancies. It is always better to reject an unqualified candidate than risk your reputation. Your end goal is to find the people who will be the right fit for your culture, match your core values, and truly move your mission forward.

Interview to Hire Process

Pre-screening Questions:

Develop a set of pre-screening questions that focus on essential criteria, such as qualifications, experience, and alignment with your center's values. These questions help filter out candidates who may not be the right fit for your center.

Phone Interview (15-20 minutes):

Conduct brief structured phone interviews to assess your candidates' initial suitability for the position. Keep it concise but be thorough.

Assessment and Decision:

Evaluate your candidates' responses to the pre-screening questions. Identify those who demonstrate the necessary qualifications, experience, and enthusiasm for the role.

Face-to-Face Interview Scheduling:

Schedule face-to-face interviews with your candidates who successfully pass the phone interview.

Interview Questions:

Develop a set of interview questions that focus on essential criteria such as problem-solving skills, clear communication, teamwork and collaboration skills, adaptability, work ethic, and if they are a cultural fit. These questions should mostly consist of specific behavior-based questions to get a feel for who they are. Use real life scenarios that are currently happening in your childcare centers.

Face-to-Face Interviews and Additional Assessments:

Proceed with face-to-face interviews. I would recommend providing your top candidates with the current theme or unit you are teaching and having them develop a sample lesson plan or activity ideas tailored to the age group they would be working with. Additionally, consider inviting those top candidates into an actual classroom setting to observe their teaching abilities and inter-actions with the children and your other employees. During this time, remove yourself and allow your candidate and your employees to interact freely. Ask for any feedback from your team regarding your candidate's classroom interaction, engagement, and overall feel for this candidate.

1. **Reference Checks:**
   Conduct reference checks for any candidate that will be moving forward in the hiring process to confirm their qualifications and work history.
2. **Final Evaluation and Job Offer:**
   Evaluate your candidates based on their performance in face-to-face inter-views and assessments. Extend a job offer to the candidate who best aligns with your center's needs and values.
3. **Deliver Rejections Gracefully:**
   Express appreciation and thank them for their time and interest in the role. Let them know that you have selected another candidate whose qual-ifications more closely align with the requirements of the position. This is important to keep your amazing reputation. You never know what people will say in the community and if you keep your interactions positive, they may refer you to others who may need childcare or are looking for employment working with children.

Onboarding and Training

Your new hires may be filled with a range of emotions in their first days starting at a new company. They made the choice to come work for you. If you want to keep your new hires, you want to keep your promises that were made during the hiring process. Building a strategic onboarding and training process will decrease staff turnover by increasing staff engagement. The journey to building the perfect team doesn't end with the hiring process; it continues through the critical phases of onboarding and training. Most of the time the terms "onboarding" and "training" are often used interchangeably; it's crucial to distinguish their separate roles in ensuring the success of your new staff members.

Onboarding

The onboarding process is the first impression a new employee has with your company. This is the time to integrate a new team member into your culture, core values, and the operational aspects of your childcare center. It is crucial to create an experience that fosters their talent and keeps them happy. We want them to settle into your center with ease. Remember, just because someone may have experience in the childcare field doesn't mean that they understand the goals and needs of your center. Having a strong onboarding system in place with set expectations will prevent any gaps in communication or expectations.

Strive to motivate them immediately. Talk honestly about what the center's goals are and where it is now. Talk about when you are at your best as a center. The last thing you want to do is tell them how well your center is running and that everything is perfect. Eventually, reality will hit, frustration will set in, and you may lose that employee. The first six months are crucial for new employees in terms of deciding if they want to stay with your center long-term. Onboarding must be an ongoing process, not a one-time event. It should extend well beyond the first day or week, providing consistent, useful feedback through regular performance evaluations and coaching.

Retaining your new hires requires exceptional leadership. Hold your leaders accountable for providing comprehensive onboarding—skipping this critical step guarantees high turnover. Throwing your new hires immediately into a classroom without proper guidance and support is a guaranteed way to lose great employees. Invest in developing strong leaders who can onboard effectively and grow your team.

Training

Centers that invest in strong training programs have a higher profit margin. Do not leave that money on the table. A strong training program is a step-by-step structured process of equipping new and current employees with the knowledge, skills, and competencies necessary to excel in their specific roles. A strong employee training program should be a key part of your employee retention strategy. Inadequate employee training will result in high turnover rates. Ensure that you have built role-specific training of all childcare standards, rules and regulations, and what skills are expected of them. Your training cannot be one-size-fits-all. While onboarding paints the picture of your company's culture, core values, vision and mission, the training teaches specific tasks, responsibilities, and educational philosophies relevant to each position within your childcare center.

Topics you may want to include in your training program:

1. **Child Development and Curriculum:** Child development stages and milestones, practical skills required for tasks such as age-appropriate lesson plans and activities, classroom management, and positive discipline techniques.

2. **Health, Safety, and Emergency Procedures:** Health and safety protocols, first aid and CPR training, child supervision, documentation, how to handle injuries, illnesses and medication, and emergency preparedness.

3. **Customer Service:** Family engagement and effective communication, parent teacher conferences, email etiquette, hard conversations, the respect of diverse family cultures and backgrounds and how to accommodate them.

4. **Technology:** Online tools, software, or documentation systems used within your center.

5. **Guidelines:** All employees must adhere to all regulations, licensing, health, and ethical standards.

6. **Professional Development and Growth:** Training resources that are available, continuing education opportunities, how goals are set to accomplish this growth, employee evaluation process.

7. **Hands On and Mentor Training:** SHOW-OBSERVE-FEEDBACK—Job shadowing to *show* what best practices look like. Observe how best practices are performed. Give consistent guidance and feedback on performance.

By recognizing the differences and implementing both onboarding and training effectively, you will create the strongest foundation for the success of your entire team. This approach will build a team that has the best work ethic and aligns with your culture, core values, mission, and vision. By taking the time to create these programs, you will equip your team with everything they need to perform at their highest capacity.

Employee Retention

Employee retention is the practice of keeping good employees with the company for as long as possible, which is impacted greatly by your policies and culture. Creating and implementing an employee retention plan will help reduce your turnover. So many childcare centers focus most of their attention on their hiring processes and not enough time on strategies to retain their employees. Losing your employees is expensive. The cost of losing an employee may cost 1.5 to two times their annual salary to replace them. That does not even account for the time and resources that go into hiring, onboarding, and training.

Turnover impacts team morale and can become very contagious. If one of your employees leaves, you have a higher risk of other employees leaving as well. The smaller capacity of the center, the higher the risk. In smaller centers, everyone relies on each other a little more, and their absence is immediately felt. Being short just one employee can lead to increased stress and potential burnout. Additionally, the close-knit feel of smaller teams means that when someone leaves, it can have an increased emotional impact, turning the sense of camaraderie and stability into uncertainty. This sense of loss and added pressure can make other employees more likely to consider leaving, creating a cycle of turnover that can be challenging to break. In higher capacity centers, turnover still poses challenges, but the impact of one employee leaving may be more easily managed with a larger team. The bigger team you have, the more likely you can spread out the responsibilities which will help relieve some of the stress and emotional impact on all other employees. It may only affect the room that the employee was in and not the entire center.

It is important to be intentional with your business planning and all the ways you can strengthen and grow your company. Create a strategic plan that you can focus on to ensure your employees feel valued and motivated to build long-term careers within your company. Prioritize developing comprehensive programs that support your employee growth, engagement, and job satisfaction. By making employee retention a core focus, you invest in the foundation of your company's success and longevity! So many childcare owners or leaders will tell me that they do not want to spend a ton of money on training their employees because they know they will just leave anyway, making it will be a waste of money. My question to you is "What if they stay?" You need to give them every fresh new shiny tool for their toolbelt so they can be the best they can be when they are working for you! You do not want your team equipped with rusty tools or no tools at all.

Here are a few strategies that you can put in place to create a work environment where your employees will feel valued, be engaged, and stay motivated for long-term employment with your company!

1. **Check in with your employees regularly**

   This will give you the insight into what people love about working for your company and what you can do to make their experience even better. Ask questions like:

   - What do you look forward to most when you come to work every day?
   - What is your favorite and least favorite aspect of your position?
   - Would you recommend working for our center? Why or why not?
   - If you were in my shoes, what would you do differently to run a more successful center?

2. **Create value for your employees to stay**

   This will be a unique combination of benefits and opportunities that make your company the best place for your employees to work. These benefits will always be the answer to the question of whether your employee stays or not. Creating these opportunities *and* following through with what is promised will decrease your employee turnover substantially. Areas of benefits and opportunities to think about:

   a. ***Competitive compensation and bonus opportunities:*** Competitive pay along with performance-based bonuses will create a sense of being valued and appreciated. When your employees feel they are recognized and rewarded for the job they are doing, they will be motivated to stay.

   b. ***Benefits***: Regularly review to ensure you are getting the best price and the plan fits who you are hiring. Examples are health, dental, vision, and retirement plans, as well as discounted childcare options.

   c. ***Professional development and growth opportunities***: Create a culture of continuous learning by offering a variety of workshops, conferences, and training opportunities to enhance your team. This will keep them updated on the best practices in the early childcare field. I also challenge you to find and provide personal development for your team to help them fulfill their goals and dreams.

d. ***Work-life balance*:** Offer flexible work schedules where possible. Ex: Job sharing, part-time, swapping schedules with others, etc. When your employees can take the time off they need, this will reduce burn out and lessen the stress they have at work and home.

e. ***Recognition and rewards*:** Acknowledge and celebrate your employees' accomplishments and achievements through reward certificates, small gifts, professional development opportunities to reinforce the value of their dedication to your center.

f. ***Employee well-being and goal setting*:** Have designated check-ins with each employee to see what you can do to help them be the best they can be. Implement wellness programs, mental health support, access to budget planning, and provide stress management options. When you focus on the overall health, wellness, and happiness of your team, you will have a team of extremely dedicated employees.

3. **Effective transparent communication**
   Establish open and transparent communication within your center. Inform all employees of any changes with rules, regulations, policies, processes, staffing updates, new families, etc. Encourage open feedback regularly. Listen to your employees' concerns and follow up with how you will be addressing these concerns. When employees are heard and are well informed, it builds trust and loyalty.

4. **Career path development**
   Work collaboratively with your employees to create individualized career development plans. Provide opportunities for advancement within the organization, whether through promotions or expanded responsibilities. This is where you can get creative with new job titles with more responsibilities.

By integrating these retention strategies, you will create an environment where your employees not only feel professionally fulfilled, but emotionally connected. At the end of the day, a satisfied and engaged team provides higher quality care for the children. Happy and motivated employees are also more likely willing to create a positive and enriching learning environment in your childcare centers.

Conclusion

Please remember, your team is the core of your childcare center's success. The employees you hire and retain will create the experiences and development of the children in your care.

By taking the time to implement strong plans and create comprehensive onboarding and training strategies, you are investing in building a team of passionate, skilled professionals dedicated to creating a strong foundation for every child and family that becomes a part of your center.

Remember, your employees are more than just babysitters; they are role models who play a significant part in a child's first years of growth and development. A strong, cohesive team aligned with your center's core values, mission, and vision is of utmost importance to providing exceptional care that exceeds the expectations of the families that choose your center.

Prioritize hiring individuals who represent the qualities you are specifically looking for— patience, creativity, a love for teaching, and a genuine commitment to child development. Develop the growth of your employees through continuous training opportunities, and foster an environment where they feel valued, supported, and motivated to build long-term careers within your center.

The investment you make in recruiting, building, and retaining an excellent team will create the childcare center that you have always dreamed of. By making your team a top priority, you are ensuring that your center operates at the highest standards of quality, providing a safe, enriching, and nurturing environment. You will feel amazing that you are creating a space for every child to learn, grow, and thrive in their early years.

Meet Aleta

With over twenty-eight years of experience in early childhood education, Aleta has held the roles of teacher, director, owner, and coach. Starting from scratch, she learned through hard lessons and perseverance, mastering business systems, marketing, leadership, and more. She grew a profitable business during a recession, expanded to four locations, and launched two complementary businesses addressing staffing challenges that everyone was facing in childcare. Her success came from surrounding myself with strong mentors and leaders, which pushed her further than she could have achieved alone. Now, she feels blessed that she gets to help business leaders and decision-makers in various industries implement strategic plans and achieve their goals through coaching and specialized services.

Aleta can be reached at aletamechtel.com

Chapter 18

Serving and Loving—Thoughts on Leadership

By Tom Wood

Tom Wood is a caring leader of people with many years experience in managing companies and teams. He works with teams in the early education space in presenting HINGE's Leadership Sprint series, which he developed and delivers passionately and with great energy and fun!

Leadership development investment is like buying fertilizer.

Before we venture into the topic of leadership itself, let's discuss what quite possibly may be the greatest challenge to you as a leader or business owner to invest in your team to improve their leadership skills. As a leader or business owner, one of your priorities, hopefully, is paying attention to the Return on Investment (ROI) with everything you spend your money on. The challenge with investing in leadership development is that this investment is like purchasing fertilizer!

By this, I mean that typically the resources we spend on leadership development do not typically come with an immediately measurable ROI. In other words, a measurable and satisfying ROI to a business owner is like the immediate results and gratification of mowing the lawn, whereby we can enjoy the results the same day sitting on the porch with a cold drink in hand.

However, fertilizer is typically purchased and spread throughout the yard with no immediate results. Shortly thereafter, we might even question why we purchased the fertilizer in the first place. However, in the future, you'll notice that the yard looks lush and green.

And so it is with the development of your current and future leaders. One may initially question the resources spent on the leadership development "fertilizer," but at a certain point in the future, the results are visible. Examples of the visible results in the individuals are:

- A more productive, results-oriented leader.
- A more motivating and motivated leader.
- A more productive and mature reaction by your leader to an immediate challenge.
- A more encouraging demeanor from your leader with teammates at all levels.
- Leadership development "fertilizer" will also impact your company!

Higher Morale

Investing in your most important asset—your people—shows you care about them not only professionally, but also personally. There is not a leadership topic that cannot be applied away from work. The message to the person that "we care about you at work and away from work" resonates and typically results in a happier and more productive team member.

Greater Employee Retention

The same love and care of the team member discussed will also typically result in that person staying with the company despite other opportunities that might come their way. Team members want to be cared for and developed as professionals and people.

Greater Ability to Attract New Talent

Here is a fact. . . Word gets around! People talk about work often, whether positive or negative. Give them something positive to talk about, since people are more likely to initiate negative chatter.

Positive Reputation in the Community

Word travels fast! The same positive "chatter" discussed travels throughout communities, neighborhoods, and families. The resulting effect is that more people want to work there, and more families want to enroll their children there. This provides a great marketing message to prospective employees and customers.

Leadership Defined

The term leadership development is often overused in this day and age, can be defined in many different ways, and is often difficult to understand. We define leadership here simply with two words: serving and loving. Although this definition may sound soft, it is anything but soft. When we are in a leadership position and have authority, either professionally or personally, and we serve and love those over whom we have authority, we demand the best from them. When we want the best from them, oftentimes we must squeeze, which can be uncomfortable! Squeezing the best out of someone is serving and loving them. When we serve and love those we have authority over and get the best *from* them, it is the best thing *for* them!

For those whom we have little or no authority over, we can still serve and love them. Serving and loving those we have no authority over is wanting and helping them to be better to the extent that they will allow themselves to be. This could be in the form of giving great advice, doing things for them, and being there when they need us. This could be as easy as bringing your elderly neighbor's newspaper to their front door from the road every morning. That is serving and loving.

In any event, and whether we are in a professional or a personal situation, great leadership is about not wanting credit and is not about taking credit. This was summed up beautifully by Lao Tzu, a fifth century BCE Chinese philosopher who said, "When the leader's work is done, the people say, 'we did it ourselves.'"

Along these lines, Leadership is also all about the position of our lens. We all have lenses. We should ask ourselves as leaders and reflect on where our lens is looking. Is it turned inward toward ourselves too much and not only when it needs to be, or is it turned outward when it needs to be toward others? It does need to be turned inward at times since we have responsibilities, However, be aware of the position of your lens, because it is not possible to serve and love others with an inward facing lens.

153

My encouragement to you is to be not only good at serving and loving others but great! We should, however, remind ourselves that to be great at anything, we never drift into it. In other words, we never drift into greatness.

I am reminded about drifting when I think about swimming in the ocean. If being great is being directly in front of my umbrella, chair, friends, and family, I have to swim against the current to remain in front of them. If I pay no attention to the current, I look up and it has carried me miles down the beach, without effort by me.

Please remember that the current always carries us away from greatness. Greatness requires effort. Swimming against the current requires effort. If we put forth no effort, the current will always carry us where we do not want to go.

And so, it is with anything we want to accomplish, whether it is a 10K race, a triathlon, being a better person, or anything that requires behavior change. Please remember that behavior change is doing something different, which is imperative for improvement towards greatness. Doing more of something, less of something, doing something new, or stop something we have been doing. Remember, becoming great is about behavior change.

Leadership Foundations

To achieve greatness in Serving and Loving others and to win the battle against the current, please remember the following foundations. As you read, please know that we will never be perfect at any of these foundations. The encouragement to you is to work on getting slightly better each day, each week, each month, etc.

Your A and A+ Game

When you work and have authority, you expect yourself and your team to bring their A game (your game of excellence) to work. You would not be in the leadership position that you are in if this was not the case. When you leave work and go to your life away from work, hopefully you bring your A+ game.

Saying that, while your A game at work is important, you're A+ life away from work is more important. Ask yourself, if someone were watching, would they say that about you?

Whether we like it or not, our A Game and A+ Game are connected. We do not live two lives. We live one life with two pieces on the same circle.

Accordingly, our A Game and our A+ Game affect and influence one another. If we do not have our A Game at work, we will not have our A+ Game away from work. If we do not have our A+ game away from work, we will not have our A Game at work. Your A and A+ games are connected, and they always will be, every day of your life. Both influence and impact the other.

Remember the impact, both positively and negatively, that the A and A+ games can have on each other. To be great at work, we should strive for greatness away from work. To be great away from work, we should strive for greatness at work. Please, however, do not confuse your quality of work with the amount of time you spend at work. It might be easy to think that since my A+ Game is more important; I should spend more and more time away from work. However, this is not a question of the time you spend at each, it is a question of what are you going to do with the time that you have?

What quality will you bring to your A Game at work every day? This typically is the majority of most of your days. What quality will you bring to your A+ Game away from work each and every day? These A+ opportunities are those small slivers of time that you have before and after work.

As a Leader, determine those things that you can do that best help you bring that A and A+ game. There are many days coming home from work when we are extremely exhausted and oftentimes frustrated. When you get home, it usually helps to turn the car off, sit for a few minutes and look at the door you are getting ready to go through while reminding yourself what is behind that door and how important it is. It will not work every day, but it is a good reminder to help you approach your A+ game with the goal of being great, and "swimming against the current" as you walk through the door. As a reminder, the "current" often will take you to just wanting to get away from the workday and getting away from everything that is behind that door. It is the same with your "work door". Always remember that when you walk through either of these doors, it's Showtime!

Further evidence of your A Game and A+ Game being connected is that there are things that you can do with each that positively (or negatively) affect the other. Among other things, being very organized in your A Game at work is of great benefit to your A+ Game. Taking great care of yourself in your A+ Game away from work (also known as Serving and Loving Yourself…. more on that later) will of great benefit to your A game at work. Accordingly, since the A and the A+

Games are connected, constantly be looking for ways that both the A and the A+ Game can support each other.

You Are Not There Yet, and You Never Will Be

You never arrive as a leader. Quite possibly the worst characteristic of a leader is when they feel like they know everything and there is nothing more to learn. We as leaders should always be looking in the mirror to determine where we can grow and what we can do better. Otherwise, we will never achieve maximum success in serving and loving anyone in our lives. What would the mirror say to you if it could talk? What areas of improvement would it say that you need as you serve and love those in your professional and personal life?

Bring the Sunshine as a Leader

Great leaders bring enthusiasm—sunshine—to their professional and personal worlds. Enthusiasm is simply defined as energy and excitement. Please know that during many of your days of serving and loving, you will not feel like bringing enthusiasm, sunshine, or any ray of light to the occasion. But great leaders strive to bring enthusiasm and sunshine, regardless of how they feel.

Sunshine as a leader can be displayed many ways. First of all, be present. Your presence as a leader is meaningful to your family, friends, and your team. Sunshine presence can be something as simple as a "Good morning," "How are you doing?" or "How was your weekend?" As a leader, please do not underestimate the impact of your presence.

As you are present and want to turn the sunshine up a notch, never forget the value to everyone around you in hearing their names. Get into the habit of using people's names in every area of your life, whether you know them well or you have just met. This is a great and seemingly simple way to serve and love others. Some of us are natural in using people's names, however, many of us must work at it.

Please remember that many individuals who serve us in our lives away from work either tell us their names or have a name tag (servers in restaurants or cashiers at grocery stores, to name a few). You might be the only person that day who honored them by calling them by their name. People love to hear their names! That is a simple way to serve and love.

An additional point on your built-in and ready-to-use sunshine—please remember that it is contagious! As a leader, you have some degree of control of the weather in any room or situation you are in. You know people that suck the life out of the room just by entering. Be that leader, whether you have authority or not, who brings the sunshine to every situation.

A final reminder, often you are not going to want to bring the sunshine. Create sunshine from the thunderstorm. Remember, we never drift into greatness, particularly with our sunshine. This type of sunshine does not rise on its own!

We've Got This!

Leaders should attempt to bring confidence to their worlds at work and away from work. Confidence is simply defined as taking fear out of the future. A confident leader uses the words "We've got this!" often. Remember that when you as a leader use these words, there is typically a part of your brain that has no idea how "we've got this" yet. Be the leader who casts that confident vision, particularly in the face of challenges. That is who others want to follow.

Also remember that there is not a bow or happy ending after every "we've got this." However, there is never a bow at the end of a challenge when a leader does not have a "we've got this" attitude.

As a Leader, You Set the Norms

Great leaders consistently display integrity. Integrity is defined as uprightness of character or simply doing the right thing. As someone with authority either at work or away from work, you set the norms. Also, in situations where your authority is limited or non-existent, you still have some degree of control over what's normal. In other words, what others see you doing as a leader is normalized. If those under your authority see you cutting corners, it will be normal for them to cut corners. Also, your actions away from work set the normal, particularly in situations where you have authority.

Your family, friends, and team are watching. What they see from you is what you will get from them! In other words, your teams, family, and friends (particularly if you have any level of authority), may do what you say, but are very likely to do what you do!

Do I Really Want to Know?

Great leaders actively seek feedback. Seeking feedback professionally or personally requires humility and vulnerability simply because many leaders are afraid of what they might hear. Ask your team, family, or friends how you can serve and love them better. The more you ask, the more comfortable they will become giving it. And the more you positively react with a thankful heart to the feedback that you get, the more they will be comfortable giving it.

As you receive feedback of any sort, whether you asked for it or not, and whether it is constructive or not, the first thing to remember to do is to *get past your first emotion*. Our first emotions when receiving constructive feedback are rarely productive. To get past your first emotion, take a breath, pause, step back, and think about what was said or written. First of all, your pause might reveal that the feedback was more valid than it originally seemed. Secondly, the pause will allow you to respond more professionally and positively, regardless of if the feedback was valid or not. The "power of the pause" is a great tool for leaders in many situations.

Finally, accept positive feedback graciously and thankfully. Realize that great feedback is also a learning experience that tells us "Do more of this!" As you accept it, be thankful, move on, and do not deflect it to something or someone else. Receiving feedback with gratitude and not deflecting is a sign of humility and strength, not arrogance.

Do THEY Really Want to Know?

Great leaders are great at giving feedback. Let's start with giving great constructive feedback. Again, either professionally or personally.

Great constructive feedback should be specific. Never give vague feedback such as "You have a bad attitude." If you feel that someone has a bad attitude, point out to them specific observations that have caused you to think that.

When a great leader gives constructive feedback and wants the team member to continue to be on the team, the leader should point out the "why." You might say, "We're having this conversation because I want you to be as successful as you can possibly be at this company." Or away from work, you might say, "We're having this conversation because I want to strengthen our relationship."

As you give feedback, remember to be thoughtful and intentional what you are going to say, respectful about who they are and their feelings, and thorough, saying everything you want to say and not stopping short. In situations where someone asks *you* for feedback, add to this a posture of being thankful. Be thankful that you are being asked for feedback—the person asking wants to serve and love you better.

You Are Awesome and I Want Everyone to Know!

Great leaders are those who often give *unsolicited compliments* to individuals on their team and in their world. Unsolicited compliments are solid gold, whether you have authority or not. Most leaders have great room for improvement in giving unsolicited compliments, though giving an unsolicited compliment may not solve your immediate problems. When we give unsolicited compliments, our lens is turned fully outward, which can be challenging. Leaders, with so much responsibility, often walk with lenses focused inward in order to focus on:

- Me First
- The Team
- The Company

Great leaders are aware of their lenses, check them often, and work to focus on:

- The Company First
- The Team
- Me

As a final note on giving compliments, think of the times you have had a conversation with a professional colleague or personal friend and complimented someone else without them being there. What are you going to do with that chunk of gold? Are you going to keep it to yourself, or are you going to share it with that person?

Sharing it is positive gossip. Be a leader professionally and personally who is a raging positive gossiper!

It Is About the Team!

Great leaders are also great team builders and teammates.

Let's talk first about being a great team builder. Great team builders need to remember that a great team starts with them.

Brace yourself for this. Great teams, culture, and leadership do not flow from the top. This is so true and possibly shocking to you. Here is the truth. Great teams' culture and leadership do not flow from the top, they ooze from the top. By that, it means that great teams, culture, and leadership are built one spoonful at a time.

One reaction at a time.

One bag of fertilizer at a time.

One sunshine delivery at a time.

One "We've got this" at a time.

One great normal at a time.

One great feedback moment at a time.

One compliment or positive gossip at a time.

On the flip side, bad culture flows downward truckloads at a time. It is amazing how much one bad decision or action by a leader can undo many great leadership oozes.

Building a great team includes casting a great, specific, and bold vision. When you build a vision, you should be clear on the vision itself and the *why*. In other words, why are we doing this and where are we going? The other important piece of clarity with a vision is that each person on the team clearly understands their role, the importance of their role, and how each of them will individually contribute to the success of achieving the vision.

As you create great teams, remember that you are also a teammate! Being a great teammate is about your focus being on what you can do to make each and every member of the team the most successful they can be. As we have discussed, and as much as you can, place your lens first on the company, then the team, then on yourself. This approach does not mean that your level of authority is diminished. The question to consider is: what you are going to do with the authority that you have?

Being a great teammate is also about stepping in and helping when you can. You may realize that you are extremely busy, but regardless of your level of authority, know that even one single occurrence of a leader stepping in and actually doing and helping with the work of their team is powerful. A great way to determine the need is to ask: "How can I help?" Once the team begins to see the leader stepping in as a great teammate, this is contagious as well.

If you have authority, remember that this becomes the normal. Jump in, help, and reward this type of behavior when you see it, since members of your team are much more likely to exhibit behaviors they observe from you and behaviors they are rewarded for doing.

What About Me?

Serving and loving in our professional and personal lives is difficult. It is swimming against the current. It can be complicated and messy. It is not something we drift into.

Now that we have established something you already know, we should prepare ourselves in the best way possible to be great at serving and loving.

To do that, we must serve and love ourselves at an extremely high level. Simply put, the better we serve and love ourselves, the better we will serve and love others. And no, this is not just about diet and exercise.

While that is part of it, there are many ways to serve and love ourselves. Some are counterintuitive, and most have "now" and "later" components to them, which typically clash with one another and say completely different things to us as we are deciding what to do.

Start Your Day Off Right

At the risk of being random, the first thing a basketball coach tells players they must do when shooting is "set your feet" before you shoot. Your morning routine is "setting your feet" before you start your day. This looks different for everyone, so determine what works best for you. Remember your morning routine is not only preparing you to have a great A Game at work, but also it puts your A+ Game on full display during that morning sliver of the time that you have before you leave your home.

You might go to the gym. You might meditate or have a spiritual time. You might (and hopefully do) eat a nutritious breakfast. You might spend quality time with a loved one. You might do it all!

Your "now" and "later" might say the following:

Now: "I just really need more sleep."

Later: "If I make the time to set my feet, I will strengthen relationships, myself and my A and A+ games today and in the future!"

Do Things for Others

When we do things for others, it is so good for *us*! Yes, your actions benefit those you help, but there is also just as much—or more—benefit for us. Think about a time you did something for someone else and how it made you feel.

Remember that you typically do not have to look for things to do for others. All you need to do is pay attention! Opportunities come to us many times each day. Pay attention and help! Your "now" and "later" might say the following:

Now: "They don't really need me to help and besides, I'm in a hurry."

Later: "Make their day and maybe make a new friend, which will be so good for me, strengthen relationships and boost my A and A+ games today and in the future!"

Connect With Others

A simple question to consider: who is that person or people who every time their name comes up, you say "you know, I need to give them a call." Well, give them a call!

In the last season of your life, long after your job is over, regardless of how it looks and where you are, there will be only one thing that matters: relationships! Connect with others. Rekindle old relationships. Start new relationship. Make the call!

Your "Now" and "Later" might say the following:

Now: "I just do not have the time right now. And besides, I am tired."

Later: "I want my last season of life (and now) to be rich with friendships and relationships, plus strengthen my A and A+ games today and in the future!"

Keep Learning New Things

What are you learning that is new and fresh at the moment? It could be something complicated like quantum physics on the side, or something fun like pottery, cooking or pickleball. Sorry, physics folks, that just does not sound fun!

Learning new things is so good for us. It opens and exercises our mind. It gives us a new confidence and is such a great way to serve and love ourselves. Your "now" and "later" might say the following:

Now: "This is going to be too hard. Besides, I am busy enough at the moment."

Later: "Learning this will give me extra courage and confidence, plus strengthen my A and A+ games today and in the future!"

Practice Gratitude

Practice is a verb that we do. It is often challenging to practice gratitude since thoughts tend to roam toward what we want and do not have. If you want to be happier, be grateful for what you have *now*. If you are in a "waiting to be grateful" state at present and are waiting for whatever you want, when you get it, you will immediately shift to what is next. Be grateful now for the great things in the now.

Practicing gratitude comes in many forms. Great ways to practice gratitude are gratitude journals, gratitude notes, compliments (a form of gratitude), being solution-oriented rather than complaint-oriented, or simply telling someone thank you.

In summary, know that happier does not live in the house of "the next thing." Happier lives in the house of now. Your "now" and "later" might say the following:

Now: "Just as soon as I get (fill in the blank), I'll be grateful."

Later: "I want to start a long-term trajectory of practicing gratitude and get away from what is sometimes a sour attitude, and strengthen my A and A+ games today and in the future."

Take Care of Yourself

You knew the diet and exercise portion of serving and loving yourself was coming, and here it is. Take care of yourself, however that looks for you. Live a healthy lifestyle, however that looks for you.

Your "now" and "later" might say the following:

Now: "Is it 5:00am already? It's cold outside and I don't want to get up."

Later: "I want to honor my ten year plan and be great in the future, plus strengthen my A and A+ games now and in the future!"

(Author's note on my ten year plan: At this point in my life, I am able to kick the soccer ball with my granddaughters. I take care of myself each day so I can still do these activities years from now. Everything I do to take care of myself is through a lens of how I want myself and my life to look ten years from now. And there is nothing wrong with the occasional cheeseburger!)

Final Words

As you reflect on leadership, please do not overthink everything you feel like you need to do and know that many or most leadership behaviors are not complicated (occasionally difficult to implement, but not complicated). Also, remember that typically the magic in serving and loving those in our professional and personal lives resides in those small moments with your lens outwardly shining bright!

Great leadership is also not about being perfect. We will never arrive at perfection. Great leadership is swimming against the current each and every day to get better. You *will* have bad days. As you reflect on the rearview mirror when you have bad days, learn from it and don't dwell on it. Give yourself some grace. There will always be the gift of tomorrow.

As you serve and love those in your professional and personal lives, please never forget the honor and privilege it is to do so. We should all strive, as we lead, to move from "I've *got* to serve and love" to "I *get* to serve and love"! Please never forget the joy of leadership!

Now, hop on your raft, swim against the current, and be great at serving and loving!

Meet Tom

Tom Wood is a strong advocate of you—the heroes in the early childhood education world who each and every day serve and love your teams, your children, and their families. In his forty-three-year career, Tom has had the privilege of working in banking, family-owned businesses, and full-time coaching and leadership development. Throughout this time, Tom has been honored to establish countless relationships, be lifted up by great leaders, and aspire to lift others up as their leader. Finally, Tom's greatest honor is being a husband of over forty years, a father and father-in-law to two amazing children and their spouses, and Pop-Pop to four beautiful granddaughters.

Tom can be reached at twood@hingeadvisors.com.

Chapter 19

Own It! Treating Employees like Owners

By Thad Joiner

Thad Joiner has developed and sold two early education companies and, in my opinion, is a master at incentivizing and elevating teams toward achieving a common goal. As the team at HINGE have supported Thad, we have come to greatly respect his ability to develop reward systems that change the lives of those he works with.

Most owners are too cheap, selfish, or lazy to treat their employees like owners. I am sharing a few of my secrets because the few of you who aren't will truly change the world.

One of my favorite comedians, George Carlin—God rest his soul—was an extremely intelligent person who told extremely intelligent jokes that had many lessons. I'd be willing to bet that he didn't realize I would use one of his jokes for years when training employees, managers, and business owners on how to treat your employees.

The joke was a supermarket joke. It had to do with cashiers and the fact that when he was waiting in line one day, every time the cashier would check somebody out, they would tell the customer, "Have a nice day." Each customer that would come through, the cashier would repeat, "Have a nice day." This would be repeated over and over again.

He would go on, saying, "Just one time I'd like the cashier to say to the customer, 'Have a crappy day.'" It was funny because he was telling us that the cashier didn't really care what type of day the customer was having. All they really cared about was doing exactly what they were trained to do: smile and say, "Have a nice day." Period.

My question is, "What do you expect from the lowest paid employee in the entire grocery store?" The cashier is the most important point of contact between the customer and the business. They are the person who could talk the longest with the customer and is the last person who has a chance to make a winning impression on that customer and ensure they return. Why is that person the lowest paid person? Why is there no incentive for that person? Why would they do a good job, and why would they care if the customer has a nice day or not?

It's a great question, it's a great story, and it's a great joke. You see, excellent customer service is rare because most business owners fail to reward workers for giving great service. The typical business out there hires a person to do a job, pays them a flat wage, and gives them little or no incentive to go the extra mile for the customer. In that climate, what happens to an employee over time? They get an attitude of indifference. Why are they trying to make the company more money? Why would they try to create more business? Think about it.

The more business created for the company, the more work a flat wage earner has to do. The incentive works in the wrong direction for a cashier. They don't want to be busy because the busier they are, the harder they have to work for the same amount of money. It's a wild concept of which, for some reason, most business owners do not seem to be conscious.

I worked at a grocery store from when I was sixteen to eighteen, initially hired as a bagger at the lowest wage possible. I was walking customers and spending quality time with them all the way to the car. When I was promoted to cashier, I became the main point of contact for that customer, the first one they got to talk to and look in the eye as they spent their hard-earned money that they had earned that week. Then I was promoted to stocker. When I became the stocker, I got a $3/hour raise. I was paid more for putting groceries on the shelves, paying no attention to the customers, than I was to actually spend time with that customer. It surprised me.

Early in my career, I became a partner manager opening up Golden Corrals throughout the city of Atlanta. Our owner came to me and said, "Well, your new wage is $30,000 a year. However, you're also going to get 10% of whatever the bottom line is each and every month." As a young professional, I thought, "Okay, that sounds good." In the very first month, we made something like $5,000, and a week later, after the financial statement was out, I was given a $500 bonus. Unbelievably excited, I went to dig apart the P&L, trying to figure out how to do better.

I quickly learned that more sales and more customers meant more money to the bottom line, and I quickly tried to put everything in place to make as much money as we possibly could. The next month, the restaurant made $10,000, and I had a $1,000 bonus. I thought, "If I can do this every month, I'm going to make $12,000 more a year. But I think I can do even better." Over the course of that year, I increased sales from $2.5 million to over $4.5 million, and our bottom line went from $10,000 a month to sometimes reaching $100,000 a month. I quickly went from making $40,000 a year with bonuses to reaching $200,000 a year. Do you think my owner was upset paying me $200,000 a year when my restaurant was putting down almost a million dollars a year to the bottom line?

Through this experience, I learned the power of capitalism and the real power of making employees and your managers owners in your business. If you want your employees and managers to act like owners of your business when you're away, then you'd better treat them like owners in how you pay them. Period.

This is what Kathy asked me to write about for this book. I could not be more excited to continue to share this message that I've been preaching and yelling from the highest of mountains to anybody who would listen for the last ten years. But the real questions I get after I speak on the local circuits and national circuits from the owners who understand: "How do I do it?"

My easiest answer is to please not complicate it. It's much easier than you think. I'm going to give you these first three things that you should ask yourself to treat employees like owners:

1. Do I want to make more money?

That sounds funny because nearly everybody does. But the simple answer is, if you want to make more money and you're a business owner, it's not going to come from you working harder. It's going to come from your valued employees doing their job, touching that customer. Go back to the supermarket story. If you want to make more money in a grocery store, then the people who manage those moments of truth, those interactions with customers, the ones who actually touch the customers every day or multiple times every day, have to be your "owners."

Most companies spend ten times more money on attracting new customers than they do on keeping the ones they have. What you need is that cashier or that bagger, the one who is interacting with the customer, to do everything they can to ensure that the customer comes back.

I used to say that if everything went to crap and I needed to go back to work, I would wait tables. Because I could not only ensure that the customer would come back, but that they would come back to the restaurant and ask for me. If I did nothing but wait on regular customers every day and almost never had to wait on new customers because my regular customers would fill my section and only want me to take care of them, I would make a lot of money waiting tables.

So, it's the same thing: if you want to make more money, then you are going to have to incentivize your team to make you more money, which means you've got to pay them like that. So, the first question I told you to ask is, do you want to make more money? If the real answer is yes, then open up your mind for question number two.

2. Would I like to work less?

The answer for most business owners is their dream is that their company runs like a machine whether they're there or not. Well, the only way to ensure that is for you to have an amazing team "owners" because someone with an owner-type mentality has to work in your business and own your business every single day. And if you're going to have people who work for you like that, you're going to have to incentivize them in some way to behave that way. It's common sense. So, the obvious answer to this is yes.

3. Do I want my employees and managers of my business to make more money?

The third one is a tough one. My obvious answer is, heck yes! I want my employees to make as much money as humanly possible. I want my employees to be paid better than any employees in the world. I want them to be the best employees in the world.

Think about it. I read recently that in 2024, the summer program at Goldman Sachs had over 380,000 applications for 3,000 internships. Do you think they got the best of the best? Absolutely. People apply for the Goldman Sachs internship because it is the highest producing and best-paid internship in the world. If you graduate from that program, you can pretty much write your ticket.

I want the best of the best lining up to work for me. If I'm running a supermarket, I want the best cashiers in the town and the county to come work for me. And how do I do that? I have to incentivize them better than anybody else. It does not happen just through training, rules, or beating them down. It has to, at the end of the day, come from an attitude inside of my employees' and managers' hearts where they believe that that grocery store is their grocery store and that the customer is their responsibility to bring back tomorrow and have them spend more money on groceries than they've ever spent, and do it because we are the best.

So, the first three questions to ask yourself in order to open up your mind and be ready to treat your employees like owners are: Do you want to make more money? Do you want to work less? And do you really want others to make more money? Now, the answers to all those questions should be easy. If your answer is yes, keep reading. . . if not, well, I can't help you.

Now that your mind's opened up and you've answered those three questions, I'm going to give you the three steps to implement this. Nothing complicated, nothing hard, just three steps.

1. **Commit to opening your books.** If you want your employees to behave and act like owners, they need to see all the information that you have, which means open up the books. You need to have timely P&Ls and ledgers so that they can see where the money is coming in, how much money is coming in, where the money is going out, and how much is going out. What's being wasted? But the real power is that your entire team, both managers and employees, needs to see that the real power to making more money is to create more customers and create more sales. There are only two ways to create more sales: have more customers coming through the door or have them spend more money when they're there. You can tell your employees this until you're blue in the face, but the only way they'll truly understand is if you open the books and let them see it for themselves. You need to meet with them, show them the financials, and teach them how to read and impact profit and loss statements (P&Ls).

2. **Identify which employees you want to include as owners.** There are different approaches, but not everyone needs to be included at the same level. In my opinion, the most important people are your middle management (store and assistant managers), upper management, and then some level of customer service employee. Once you've identified the employee levels for ownership, decide what percentage of profits will be set aside for employee bonuses. My suggestion to business owners is to target setting aside 30% of profits for bonuses. While 30% might seem like a lot, consider this: would you rather get 95% of a small profit or 70% of a much larger profit? An incentive program that motivates managers and employees to achieve significant results is key to exponential growth.

   Figure out how to distribute the bonus pool among the included employees. Here's a suggestion:
   - 10% for upper-level management
   - 10% for the general manager/director/highest on-site manager at a location
   - 5% for an associate-level manager (maybe the second in charge)
   - 5% in a pool for customer-facing employees (you can decide how to split this further)

   There are many ways to approach this, and you can certainly get more detailed, but this gives you a basic framework. The idea for non-bonused employees is that you want them busting their humps to become one of the employees in the bonus pool. You want that number three manager who's not getting a bonus, not getting this commission, to be hungry to get that promotion. And once they get onto that bonus program, it is a huge lift for them. Now they have a story to tell.

3. **The last step is the hardest one for a business owner to understand, and it should be the easiest.** Make the bonus program easy, with no fine print and very easy to understand. Hear me again: the bonus program should not be hard to understand in any way. It should be something like "Hey listen, we're going to pay this bonus, this commission, two weeks after the monthly financial is done, and it's exactly this percentage of the bottom line."

Your "bonusable" employees should know ahead of time what the bonus will be. The biggest mistake I see business owners make is they implement a bonus plan, and they make it where the average manager or employee can't even calculate their bonus. It needs to be easy. "I made $50,000, I get $5,000. I made $100,000, I get $10,000." That's how easy it should be. I don't want there to be fine print, but whatever fine print you have, make it very easy to understand and do not, under any circumstances, put a cap on how much money they're going to get or change the bonus program because they're making "too much money." There is no such thing. You set aside a certain amount of your bottom line, and that's how much you're going to pay.

So, the first three things, once you decided that you wanted to do this after you opened your mind, were to open the books, determine your levels, and lastly, determine the (limited) fine print. It's going to be uncapped, you're going to pay it on time, and you're not going to *love* paying the bonus. Honestly, though, it really is my favorite thing to do for my employees.

Now lastly, you've done all this, and I'm going to give you three follow-ups. I've already given you three questions to ask yourself: do you want to make more money, do you want to work less, and do you want others in your system to make more money? The next three things were the three steps on how to implement, and those were to open up your books, decide the levels of employees who were going to get it, and decide your fine print, of which you were going to have very little.

The final three steps are your three steps of follow-up:

1. **Get credit.** You need to tell your employees about it so they understand how unique it is. You need to tell your customers about it. Everybody needs to know that you are treating your employees like owners. You'll get a reputation in your industry and your community for treating your employees like owners.

2. **Do not cap this.** You must make it where your employees can make an unlimited amount of money. If you make a million dollars, they get $100,000. I want it exactly like that for your upper management, your middle management, and your lower management. This is how you attract the best and retain them.

3. **Do not complicate this.** Make it where everyone can calculate it. Even the person not getting it knows. You want that number three manager to know that they're going to be getting 5% of the bottom line when they get promoted. You want them fighting for that promotion. You want them ready to transfer to another location to get that promotion to get that money. We want this to be meaningful, so make it that way.

You now have your three questions to ask yourself—you have your steps on how to implement and your three follow-ups. I'm going to give you a bonus. I found that this bonus system worked unbelievably well for me for years, and it still does. But as I have had some long-term employees and long-term partners who worked with me for years creating wealth and happiness for me, I found that what I really wanted was for them to take another step as well. And that was to actually make them owners. This was something that I prayed about and thought about for years. Then I finally did it.

I was able to gift 20% of my last company to three key employees. It was split in different ways, and they vested it differently over different amounts of time. But I think if you're really ready and you find this bonus and commission system to be successful for you, you're going to want to see the power in actually making them owners. Making them thirty-year lifetime employees that, when you sell, they participate in that, not only with getting a great salary, but now they have a full-blown cash event.

I was lucky enough when I sold my last company that I created three other millionaires. That's something I never would have imagined. I had an employee who went through this bonus program that, when she started with me, made $8.50 an hour. Ten years later, when I sold, she received $2.2 million. I created three millionaires from one event. I don't have to explain to you how their lives changed.

Here's hoping that this book and this chapter spark some change and some positivity in your business. Know that I'm always available. Reach out and find me, and I will help you in any way I can to create these programs in your business. Thank you, Kathy, for this opportunity.

Meet Thad

Thad Joiner, a proud husband and father, has over three decades of entrepreneurial success in multiple industries. Founding his first business at age twenty-one and continuing today where he is Founder and CEO of Scallions Development Company and Better Beans Branding, Thad has consistently demonstrated his expertise in growing businesses. He is an active member of his church, a Coach in his community, and an active Board Member of the Georgia Child Care Association and serves on the BOOST Advisory Board.

Thad can be reached at thad@betterbeansbranding.com.

Appendix 1
Complete Case Study

Harriet Had a Dream

Harriet had an amazing career as a university level French teacher. She values education and studied hard to reach a high level of achievement in her career. Her passion is for students to understand the value in their education and particularly to gain exposure to difference languages and cultures. When her first child was born, she took a modest maternity leave and then began looking for a high-quality learning environment for her young daughter while she worked. Although she found some options in her community that she felt would be safe and caring, she was disappointed with the options that supported her dream of having her children exposed to a diverse group of children and cultures, in stimulating environments, with a modern facility and high-quality classroom materials. Harriet decided that in order to provide all that she wanted for her daughter, she would need to create it herself! After all, she was an educator!

Harriet Developed her Company

Harriet searched for meaningful business help as she was launching her company and found some useful resources in her local small business development group and a local real estate broker. She became frustrated though that no one seemed to be able to tell her how to open an early education business and how to operate it efficiently. With big dreams, some personal savings, and a small loan from her parents, she found a building to rent and convinced the landlord to invest in the interior space and playground. Along with her personal funds and loan from her parents, Harriet took out a small SBA loan to supplement the cost of equipment, furniture, and curriculum, and to cover any start-up losses. She began to feel nervous that the secure level of income she had worked so hard to achieve in teaching was gone and that everything she had, including her family's well-being, was now at risk. She developed the curriculum herself and supplemented it with some early education resources focused on teaching a foreign language and introducing the students to a variety of cultures. Harriet took a look at local childcare centers and set her tuition rates a bit lower, wanting to attract families quickly. She decided to offer discounts to her team for their own childcare costs, and to families who were out for illness or vacation. Her local competitors didn't give a discount to families if they have more than one child enrolled in the school, so she decided not to do that either. Harriet wanted to hire the very best teachers and knew that she would need to pay them more than her competition to attract quality talent. After the extensive and exhausting processes of permitting, renovations, and licensing, Harriet was ready for business!!

Harriet Opened the Doors

The first year was a BIG challenge, but Harriet expected that! She found herself in a continual process of hiring, training, opening new classes, and juggling parent communication and staff performance issues. Harriet felt that she was falling behind in meeting parent demands and behavorial issues in the classrooms and was working from opening to closing, putting a strain on her family. She knew that she should hire a Director at some point but with her cash still not at a breakeven point, she didn't want to commit to a large salary for a Director. She found herself covering classes regularly when teachers were sick. She felt that her enrollment was strong, but she was still struggling financially. Harriet wondered what she was doing wrong?

Harriet's First Two Years

For the first year, Harriet had to go back to her parents for a second loan because she was not cash positive and found herself in a difficult catch-22. She was working twelve-hour days to help support teachers and cover classrooms, and didn't have enough information to understand why she was still struggling and wasn't even sure if she was collecting all of her money! Harriet was exhausted every day after work and waking in the middle of the night concerned about making payroll and the rent. By the beginning of the second year, Harriet attended a state childcare conference and heard Kathy Ligon, of HINGE Advisors, speak about the Five Pillars of Purpose-Driven Profit. Her initial reaction was that this person was probably crazy, because she said don't worry about salaries and rent until the school has a healthy level of occupancy!! What?!?? Don't worry about expenses?? Well not exactly "don't worry". But do your best and then focus on enrolling. And though Kathy might be crazy, she WAS old, and HAD been around the industry for a very long time. What Harriet did know was that she couldn't keep up this pace much longer. Her family was suffering and so was she. Harriet needed something different. So, she began year two with a mission to work on her business—not in it!!

Occupancy

There are three basic methods for calculating occupancy, each with increasing complexity, but also with increasing accuracy and information that allows for healthy decision making. All three methods are calculated by comparing some metric to the Licensed Capacity. I encourage the majority of business owners to use the actual Licensed Capacity and not their own internal "Effective Capacity"—meaning the number they have decided is their maximum capacity. The reason is that you could, in fact, enroll to Licensed Capacity. You might have a very good reason not to, such as group sizes when it is not cost effective to hire another teacher to add one or two enrollments to a classroom, or you feel that your level of quality isn't conducive to higher ratios, but it is important to have the information that shows you the impact of your decisions. Not that your decisions are wrong, but that they are intentional decisions that impact the financial picture in your school. So, for our calculations, let's use actual Licensed Capacity.

After learning more about the Five Pillars, Harriet decided that she didn't have much to lose in making some changes in her business practices because the cash drain could not continue! She decided to dig in and follow the best practices she had learned toward financial health. Initially Harriet believed that her school was well-enrolled as she had all of her classes open. But now, learning more about the impact of occupancy on her financial health, she thought differently about the additional space she had in each classroom for one or two new enrollments. To support that, she recently started a waitlist--one that she felt she could depend on as parents had paid deposits to secure their child's spot!

Her original fear in maximizing her ratios, was that the team would be too stressed if she added more children. Contributing to her fear was that she had lost two teachers to out-of-industry positions that were less stressful—and that made her nervous about adding more students. She went back and forth with questions in her mind . How much of an impact would a couple of students make anyway? Was she going to stress even more teachers? And at the same time ,she knew that what she was doing was not sustainable in the long run. No matter how great her intentions were.

To mitigate that risk, she decided to bring the entire staff into a conversation about what a stronger enrollment would mean to the school in the form of increased pay and benefits, as well as abundant classroom resources and advancement opportunities for the team. In addition, she worked with the team in how they could participate in enrollment by developing prospective parent tours that pointed out the unique features of the school and focused on customer service and parent engagement.

At the end of the day, Harriet was determined to make her dream a thriving business! So, she began working on the Five Pillars by focusing on Occupancy first.

Method 1. The Headcount Method

A simple headcount method is fast and easy. In this method, the number of students enrolled is compared to the Licensed Capacity.

For instance, Harriet's school is licensed for 110 students, and there are 92 students enrolled, so in her example, she will divide the currently enrolled students (92) into the Licensed Capacity (110), The result with this method is that the school is 83.64% full (92/100 = .8364).

Calculation
92 enrolled students / 110 licensed capacity = .8364 or 83.64% occupancy

What this calculation says logically is of all the children Harriet could serve in this building, she is serving 83.64% of that. There are several hidden dangers in using this method alone, but it can also be a quick gauge of increases and decreases in enrollment.

Method 2. The FTE Method

FTE, or Full-Time Equivalent, is a common method used to more accurately calculate occupancy, adding full-time and part-time enrollments into measurable full-time units. In this method, full-time students are counted as 1 enrollment, and part-time students are counted as ½ enrollment. In this method, FTE, instead of headcount, is compared to the Licensed Capacity.

For example, using the same information for Harriet above, of the 92 enrolled children, 70 are full-time, and 22 are part-time. Full-time students are counted as 1 (70 full-time) and part-time students are counted as ½ (22 part-time x ½ = 11). Adding the full-time of 70 to the part-time of 11, we get an FTE of 88. We then compare the FTE of 88 to the licensed capacity of 110, and the school is 80% full (88/110 = .8).

Calculation
88 FTE / 110 licensed capacity = .8 or 80% occupancy

This more detailed information says logically that there is greater capacity to enroll than Harriet thought under the Head Count Method as she has now considered the effect of part-time students. Before and after school populations are counted as part-time (except in holiday or summer periods) and there are times when enrollment-building means that you can be more flexible with part-time programming. Part-time students are not a bad decision and particularly useful when ramping a new or under-performing school. But when approaching maximum capacity, it is healthier to either request that part-time students begin full-time schedules, or to combine part-time programs that then equal full-time attendance (for instance, requiring either 2-day and 3-day schedules that combine for a full-week, and a higher tuition than one full-time student). Note also, in this challenging hiring environment, that part-time programs can potentially be more difficult for teachers to manage.

Accuracy increased using the FTE method by showing that Harriet's Occupancy was actually 3.64 children lower than using the Headcount Method, pointing out a greater ability to enroll. Harriet was more aware of her ability to enroll and ready to focus her time and marketing efforts toward filling those slots. She was beginning to understand the value of 3-4 more children in her program and in including her team in the strategy and helping them to grow as professionals!

Method 3. The Revenue Maximization Method

The most informative method, and one that considers all aspects of the revenue picture including tuition rates, other charges such as registration fees and late payment fees, and the effects of discounting, is what I refer to as the revenue maximization method. Simply, this method is based on what cash actually is available to meet expense obligations. At the end of the day, that is what matters the most in maintaining financial health. This method will arm you with the information you need to consider the impact of the tuition rate and discounting decisions you are making and how they impact your ability to operate. There could be hidden dangers in the more basic methods that are not uncovered using headcount and FTE methods.

In Harriet's business, the school earns $1,200,000 in net revenue annually. Net revenue is the cash available to go in the bank for paying expenses—i.e. tuition income plus other charges, minus discounts. This amount can be found easily on the Income line of your tax return, or from your billing system-- typically in some version of an annual Total Charge Credit Summary report. In our example, the school earns $1,270,000 in annual tuition income, $10,000 in other charges (initial registration fees, late payment fees, etc.) and discounts $80,000. (see Pillar Three).

Calculation
$1,270,000 tuition income + $10,000 other charges -
$80,000 discounts = $1,200,000 net revenue

Further, in Harriet's school, the average tuition rate weekly is $310. The average tuition rate for a school that serves infant through afterschool populations will typically be the three-year-old tuition rate, as infant/toddler tuition rates are usually higher, and afterschool tuition rates are typically lower. Our licensed capacity is 110.

Calculation
$1,200,000 annual net revenue / 110 licensed capacity / $310 average weekly tuition rate / 52 weeks = .6767 or 67.67% occupancy

What this says logically is of all the revenue that Harriet could earn using this facility without changing the tuition rate or licensed capacity, she is earning 67.67% of that. Using the revenue maximization method uncovered some possibilities for bringing the school into greater financial health and has revealed less than minimum financial health occupancy of 70%. At a revenue maximization occupancy of 67.67%, the school is missing some opportunities for stability. Some additional strategies might be to consider whether the tuition rates are actually covering the cost of services (See Pillar Two), or whether there is the opportunity to increase other income (see notes on other income), or if discounts can be eliminated or reduced (see Pillar Three).

But Harriet learned to focus on occupancy first, so she now decides to take a risk and hire a director that in the short run, will put her financial health at greater risk, but in the long run, will allow her to focus on enrollment building and supporting the staff to prepare for more students. And the investment paid off! After a few months, Harriet managed to enroll to 80% capacity by adding 13 additional students, and without changing the tuition rate. She now earns $1,418,500 in net revenue annually! An increase of $218,560! Harriet is starting to feel more confident in her ability to free herself up to strategize healthy business practices and to implement them in a healthy way.

Calculation
$1,418,560 annual net revenue / 110 licensed capacity / $310 average weekly tuition rate / 52 weeks = .8 or 80% occupancy

With the new enrollment, Harriet is maximizing the ability of the school to serve more families, while creating greater financial resources to hire, add pay and benefits, and possibly grow to serve more families. She quickly realized that the new enrollments were in classes where costs were already covered, making the majority of the revenue gained—except for a bit more food and supplies—complete profit! This one change meant that she was now financially stable after hiring her Director, and with the excess cash could dream of adding a new supplemental curriculum and hiring a floater to alleviate teacher burnout.

Closely tracking occupancy is critical to the success of your childcare business, and for the well-being of families and teams. Knowing the impact of your enrollment decisions on the overall financial picture is vital.

Tuition Rates and Other Income

As Harriet recently hired, she noticed that pay rates were increasing as new team members were demanding higher wages and that she was losing candidates to higher paying jobs in other industries. With the increased wages, Harriet is now spending more for salaries and wonders if she is not managing her staff hours well? Or maybe she should consider whether she is still charging the cost of care tuition rate as she has learned that issues balancing staff spending percentages could be less about too many hours, and more about not charging enough to cover her costs. Her new dreams of training her teachers in new classroom management techniques, investing in a new curriculum enhancement program, and seeking an accreditation seem out of reach as she begins to, once again, conserve cash. Harriet was successful with Pillar One and feels more confident to now consider her tuition rates.

As a reminder, Harriet's financial picture looked like this after increasing occupancy to 80%.

> ### Calculation
> $1,418,560 annual net revenue / 110 licensed capacity / $310 average weekly tuition rate / 52 weeks = .8 or 80% occupancy

What this says logically is of all the revenue Harriet could earn in this building, given the current average tuition rate, she is earning 80% of that. Harriet also knows, as she has learned, that at this level of revenue maximization occupancy, she should have abundant resources to invest in her school.

Harriet is now wondering if her original strategy to keep her tuition rates slightly lower than the local competition is actually working against her. Perhaps she is not getting the credit in the community to be considered a high-quality program and perhaps her tuition rates aren't sufficient to cover the new cost of care with recent rising pay requirements. She has seen an increase in staff salaries of 35% recently, and with the help of the Framework benchmarking tool, she calculates that she needs to increase tuition rates by 12%. Harriet considered a smaller increase to not burden her families, but now understands that she can't effectively support her teachers and cover other necessary costs that will ensure that her student will thrive unless she takes bold action. Although this new tuition rate will put her a good bit above other local operators, she knows that her high-quality program is superior, and that her team is the best! She decides, very nervously, to implement the change and hope for the best. The 12% increase will move the average tuition from $310 to $347 weekly. Harriet calculates that if she loses no enrollment, then her new financial picture will look like this:

Calculation
110 licensed capacity * $347 average weekly tuition rate * 52 weeks* 80% occupancy = $1,587,872 annual net revenue

By increasing the tuition rate for current families by 12%, Harriet will increase her Annual Net Revenue by $169,312. This cash increase could go a long way to hire additional staff, increase pay or benefits, improve the curriculum or facility, or grow to serve more children.

Another interesting calculation Harriet considered before making the change in her tuition rates was to forecast how many enrollments could be lost and not lose revenue. In our example, the answer is 9.

Calculation
$169,312 increase in annual net revenue / $347 weekly average tuition rate / 52 weeks = 9.38

Once she decided to implement the tuition rate increase, Harriet was very sad to lose a family with two children to a lower-cost option. Although she didn't want to put a strain on anyone, she understood the value in the tough decision to align her tuition rates with the actual cost of care necessary to create a thriving school. She also sees how hard her team works every day and how passionate they are about teaching and growing to serve more children and in new and creative ways. Her current waitlist meant that she quickly enrolled two new students and was happy with her decision!

The accurate setting of the tuition rate of an early education center is a powerful tool for creating the type of school and services you intend, along with communicating quality and value to parents. By setting rates that align with the quality of your services, being transparent in your communication, and staying attuned to market dynamics, you can ensure that your pricing strategy effectively reflects the excellence of your school.

Discounts

Harriet is now taking some time off and is cutting down on the amount of time she is in the school—with great success! The team is beginning to thrive and is eager to learn and grow in their roles. With the new management position and more financial health, she is able to increase pay and is finding it easier to hire and support her teachers with more time off and is sending them for advanced training. Her work/life balance feels more in line and she is sleeping much better!

After learning about how to gain accurate information to make decisions around the impact of her policy setting, Harriet began to use her billing system as a valuable tool in managing her company. She began to record the full tuition in her system and then apply a discount, recording the discount by type, so she could see clearly the impact of her discounting decisions. She now has the information that show that she is discounting $80,000 annually in a combination of $60,000 for vacation days and $20,000 for staff discounts. Harriet knows that other local providers allow families to not pay when their children don't attend, but now that she is armed with the information about how much this is costing the school, and how much she could do with the extra $60,000 a year, she decides to eliminate this discount and focus solely on discounts for her team's children. By eliminating vacation discounts, she decreases her total discounts from $80,000 to $20,000, adding $60,000 to the bottom line. The new net revenue is now $1,647,872.

> **Calculation**
>
> $1,587,872 former net revenue + $60,000 reduction in discounts = $1,647,872

What this says logically, is Harriet now had $60,000 more in cash to improve salaries, possibly add health insurance or a new curriculum, or hire a floater to relieve teachers and cover absences.

Salary Costs

Harriet's original dream was to hire the very best teachers and she knew that she would need to pay them more than her competition to attract the best ones. She also understood that hiring decisions would be among the most important ones she would make, but early on she didn't understand how hard it would be to balance her staff costs with quality programming and financial health. Before she knew to focus on occupancy to build a stronger revenue stream and eliminate discounts that were no longer industry norm, she had a terrible time controlling costs at a healthy percentage of revenue, was constantly wondering how else she could cut costs, and lacked the team she needed to adequately manage the school and focus on enrollment. Harriet was spending $695,000 annually for her team's salaries, which included overtime, holiday pay, and PTO pay. Her salary position looked like this:

> **Former Calculation**
>
> $695,000 / $1,200,000 former net revenue = .5792 or 57.92%

What this says logically is of all the revenue Harriet was earning in her school, she was spending 57.92% of that on staff salaries only.

Harriet learned that she would always struggle to have the team she needed to adequately create the high quality and stable environment she was dreaming of if she didn't figure out how to get this important metric in line. Initially thinking that she was doing something wrong with cost control, she felt that she was just running in circles analyzing pay rates, managing hours, sending staff home early, and still not having the time to focus on high quality programming and enrolling.

Once Harriet made revenue-building her focus over trying to cost-control her way out of the problem, she took a risk on hiring a director for $80,000 in annual salary, and re-directed herself to running the business, strategizing enrollment and supporting the team and families better. With the net revenue increase generated by a higher occupancy, increasing tuition rates to a cost of care rate, and eliminating some unnecessary discounts, she actually increased the salaries but was now in a more stable position.

New Calculation
$$\$775,000 \ / \ \$1,647,872 = .47 \text{ or } 47\%$$

Harriet increased salaries by the $80,000 with the new director position and was now seeing that although she was spending more, she was also earning more, and she had reduced the salary percent to 47% of net income. She knew that this was slightly higher than the targeted benchmark of 45%, and she would continue to work on strengthening her net income within the tolerance level of her customers' ability and desire to pay the cost of care tuition rate.

Harriet was on a roll! She implemented staff cost management systems that included setting staff schedules to align with children's schedules and she trained her management and teaching teams to continually monitor ratios so that someone might take advantage of the ability to go home early, saving the school resources and improving the work/life balance for those team members interested in more personal time. A win-win for all!!

Facility Costs

Harriet has worked hard to align her school's revenue stream with healthy benchmarks and is proud of all that she has accomplished! With process for continual evaluation of occupancy and enrollment opportunities, along with daily staff cost management, and semi-annual evaluation of her Tuition Rates and Discounts, Harriet wonders if her rent cost is working well for her. Her initial strategy was to be in an area that was growing with a customer base that seemed eager to invest in early education for their children, and in a facility that was visible, maximized space, and was attractive to drive-by traffic. When she started, she compared the rent to other retail spaces in the area and learned from a local broker that it was in line with the market. Now that she understood early education benchmarks, she wonders if her leased facility is working for the financial health of her business or against it. She reviewed the benchmarks and calculated the following.

Her business generated the following annual revenue at the benchmark of 70% occupancy:

110 licensed capacity * $347 average weekly tuition rate * 52 weeks * .7 or 70% occupancy = $1,389,388 annual net revenue

Her rent is $265,000 annually.

> **Calculation**
> $265,000 annual rent / $1,389,388 annual net revenue at 70% occupancy = .1907 or 19%

Harriet has now learned that true "market" rent is driven by her business's ability to pay rent, and not necessarily what other industries are paying for similar buildings in her area. Also, she understands that paying rent at 15% of 70% occupancy is a healthy benchmark. With her rent at 19% of net revenue when she is 70% full, she calculates that her rent would have created a more stable financial picture for the school if it had been in the $210,000 range.

> **Calculation**
> $1,389,388 annual net revenue at 70% * .15 or 15% rent = $208,408 in annual rent

Harriet plans to ask her landlord if she will either lower the rent in exchange for a longer-term lease, or if she will invest in an expansion of the school, or if she will help Harriet seek a second facility to expand into as Harriet now has several eager team members trained and ready for advancement opportunities! She realizes that she had grown the team well and that she is in danger of losing them unless she could continues to give them opportunities to grow. And her new director would love to eventually grow to be an area manager over several schools! How exciting!!

What Became of Harriet?

Harriet has come a long way! With a combination of maximizing enrollment and implementing a continual system of monitoring openings, increasing tuition rates to changing cost of care rates, eliminating discounts that were no longer industry norm, managing staff salaries to align with healthy metrics, and consider growth opportunities by using her landlord's resources, Harriet is ready for her second location! She was also able to take a vacation with her family this year and for the first time since starting her company, relaxed and enjoyed it. It is not just possible to create a business that allows children and staff to thrive, it is necessary!

Maybe that Kathy Ligon wasn't so crazy after all . . . . .

Appendix 2
Definitions

The **Average Tuition Rate** for a school that serves infant through afterschool populations will typically be the three-year-old tuition rate, as Infant/Toddler tuition rates are usually higher, and afterschool tuition rates are typically lower.

A **Benchmark**, by definition, is a standard or point of reference against which things may be compared or assessed.

A **Competitor** is someone providing services in your market, with the same level of programming, curriculum, and staff quality, in a facility with similar quality and the same offerings such as hours and age group served.

Effective Capacity is the capacity that a business owner chooses to serve in their facility at one time. This capacity may be less than the licensed capacity to allow for greater staff to child interaction.

Financial Health is defined as the ability to earn enough revenue to hire staff at healthy wages and support their training, retention, and benefits needs, maintain regulatory compliance, invest in high quality curriculum and supplies, develop and maintain safe and inviting facilities and learning spaces, create resources to reinvest in and grow the company, and support the owner with personal resources—all working together to create a thriving environment for the many stakeholders that the business supports.

FTE, or Full-Time Equivalent, is a common method used to most accurately calculate occupancy, adding full-time and part-time enrollments into measurable full-time units.

Licensed Capacity is the number of potential children that a facility is legally able to serve at one time.

A **Loss Leader** is selling a service at a price that is not profitable but is sold to attract new customers or to sell additional services to those customers.

Net Revenue is the cash available to go in the bank for paying expenses—i.e., tuition income plus other charges, minus discounts.

Occupancy is the percentage of available spaces filled by enrolled children and a measure of how well you are using your available space. Occupancy in its most accurate and useful form (see Pillar One), is net revenue divided by licensed capacity divided by average tuition rate divided by number of periods (52 weeks, 12 months, or 1 year) you are calculating.

Revenue Maximization Method is the most accurate and beneficial method for calculating occupancy, considering all aspects of the revenue picture including tuition rates, other charges such as registration fees and late payment fees, and the effects of discounting.

Salary Costs are calculated by dividing the weekly total salary costs into the net revenue. The weekly salary costs can be gained from your payroll system.